What is my baby thinking?

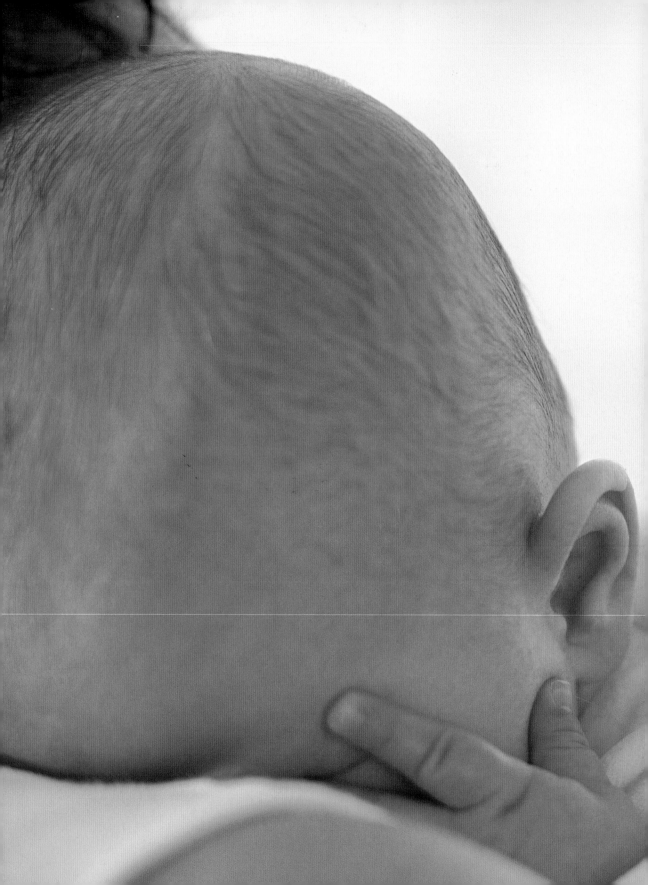

What is my baby thinking?

Understanding babies and toddlers from 0–3 years

Dr Richard Woolfson

hamlyn

First published in Great Britain in 2006 by Hamlyn,
a division of Octopus Publishing Group Ltd
2–4 Heron Quays, London E14 4JP

Distributed in the United States and Canada by
Sterling Publishing Co., Inc.
387 Park Avenue South, New York, NY 10016-8810

ISBN-13: 978-0-600-61363-3
ISBN-10: 0-600-61363-1

A CIP catalogue record for this book is available
from the British Library

10 9 8 7 6 5 4 3 2 1

Printed and bound in China

Contents

Introduction

Born to think

From the moment your baby arrives in this world, she is hard-wired to think. She is born with more than one billion brain cells (neurons) – that's 100,000,000,000 units inside her head responsible for thinking – which are interconnected by even more long, thin fibres (synapses). One single brain cell can be connected to around 15,000 others.

I'm unique

This thinking network lays the foundation for all your baby's subsequent mental development. Every baby's brain is different: just as they have different personalities and different sets of abilities, so they also have different and unique brains. The brain of your new baby has just about as many cells as yours, but not all of them are connected up so she doesn't think as well as you do. Brain growth, and growth in thinking, continues for the rest of her childhood and beyond.

Although there are no overall gender differences in brain size (when comparing boy and girl babies of equal weight and length), girls are quicker to develop the use of the left side of their brain, which is associated with speech and language skills. Girls also tend to have stronger connections between the two sides of the brain, which may explain why girls are better at multi-tasking while boys prefer to focus on one task at a time.

How your baby's brain develops

Your baby's thinking machinery began to develop even during the pregnancy. Here are some facts about pre-natal brain growth following conception:

Five weeks Cells start to divide in the embryo's forebrain region, eventually creating her two cerebral hemispheres.

Five to 20 weeks Around 50,000–100,000 new brain cells are generated every single second.

Three months Myelin – a white fatty substance that develops around the connecting wires to allow brain messages to flow quickly – grows in the spinal cord.

Six months Myelin starts to grow around the connecting wires in the embryo's brain.

Your baby's brain weighs 300–350 g (10–11 oz) at birth, depending on her overall body weight. By her third birthday, her brain has reached around 80 per cent of its final adult size, and by the age of five it has reached 90 per cent.

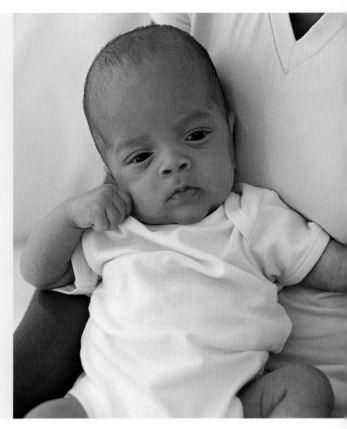

I need to think

Your baby starts to use her thinking ability from the moment she is born. The more you understand what she thinks, the better, because this will help you get to know her better, and to determine her likes and dislikes, as well as the games and activities she prefers. While the exact relationship between thought and language is unclear, even in adults, there is no doubt that your baby can think long before she speaks at all. Once she starts to use spoken words, however, thinking and language become more closely intertwined.

Yet there is another reason why it's important to know what your baby thinks. Although her brain cells are present (along with all the other neurological material needed to make detailed thinking development possible), plus the capacity to form connections between those cells, a lot of work still has to be done. The stimulation and experiences she receives during her early childhood play a huge part in developing her brain capacity. If you know what she thinks, you will know how to challenge her, how to stimulate her, and how to stretch her thinking ability even further.

We need to bond

During the early months, you and your baby are drawn together as you each get to know the other. This process of bonding – that is, the forming of a close, two-way emotional attachment between you and your baby – has a huge effect on his future emotional development. He needs to bond with you, and this need probably dominates his thinking for much of the time, especially in the early weeks.

Love me

Your baby's vision is pre-tuned to focus at around 20–30 cm (8–12 in) from the end of his nose – and that's normally the distance you hold him from your face while you feed him (whether bottle-fed or breast-fed, this distance is about the same). So he is pre-programmed to see your face while feeding, and he thoroughly enjoys this process.

Although his vision is still developing from birth onwards and he may not specifically recognize a smile until he is around two months old, your baby senses when you smile at him. He is aware of the changes in your muscle tone, as well as those in your voice. By the time he is six weeks old, he starts to reciprocate with a smile of his own.

Being held in your arms is very important to your baby – it provides him with a feeling of safety and security, a kind of human blanket that gives him comfort. Your loving physical affection when he is miserable enhances the psychological connection between you. Your ability to calm him with a hug when he is upset helps to promote his development.

Talk to me and touch me

Of course, your baby doesn't understand human language the moment he is born. However, research has found that a baby's ear is pre-tuned to hear human voices more than any other sound in the environment. Not only that, a baby typically is more sensitive to sounds that have a higher pitch, and therefore is more responsive to his mother's voice than to his father's.

One of the best ways for your baby to connect with you is through loving touch. He thrives when you gently stroke his cheek or softly kiss his hands and face. These actions make him feel good about himself and about you. Studies suggest that baby girls are more sensitive to touch than baby boys, but all babies love this contact anyway.

Tips for bonding

- Look at your baby while he drinks his milk. Whenever possible, turn your face so that it is clearly in his line of vision.
- Give your baby plenty of smiles, even though he might not respond with one of his own. He senses the emotional warmth you extend towards him.
- Do your best to cuddle your baby when he cries, even though you may not always know what is actually upsetting him at the time.
- Chat to your baby at every opportunity: when you feed him, when you change him and when you play with him. Speech enhances your relationship with him.
- While holding your baby in your arms, gently draw your fingers down his cheek or across his chin. He might kick his legs with delight!

All by myself

One of the key urges driving your growing infant forward during the first couple of years is her desire for independence – in most instances, she likes doing things by herself. The problem she faces is that her aspirations often outstrip her abilities.

I want to do it on my own

Much of the time your baby tries to take on challenges that are far beyond her skills. For instance, at eight months old she tries to pull herself into a standing position in order to reach a toy and screams when she can't do it; or at 18 months old she has a burst of temper when you try to help put the correct shape into the hole in the shape sorter.

I want it both ways

When it comes to independence, a complicating factor is that, although your child wants to manage by herself, she still likes you beside her for reassurance. No wonder there are times when you don't know what to do for the best. Your assistance is greeted with rage – and yet when you leave her to get on with it herself, she howls with frustration. Both desires compete with each other, and sometimes you just can't get it right.

Although this need for independence is inconvenient for you at times – for instance, it's easier to dress and undress your toddler yourself, rather than to wait for her to manage some of the items by herself – do what you can to encourage her to think in this way. Don't dissuade her.

Show me the way

You can support your child's drive for independence by showing her that the best way to achieve a target is in small stages, rather than in huge jumps. For instance, suppose she wants to put all the pieces back into the correct places in the wooden inset board. This is a huge challenge, because there may be six pieces, each with its own hole on the board. Make it easier by giving her only one piece at a time, and perhaps cover up four of the spaces. Then let her put the piece back by herself. In other words, whatever your toddler thinks she would like to achieve, break it down into small steps for her and then let her tackle one step at a time.

When she does reach a solution by herself, shower her with praise. She thrives on your approval and tries even harder the next time. The more success she achieves in her efforts to be independent, then the more enthusiasm she has for further progress – and remember to reassure her when she's upset by failure.

Developing independence

- Young children who are independent (compared to others of the same age) are likely to maintain that level of independence throughout later childhood and into adulthood. The drive to be self-supporting continues throughout life.
- Many 'milestones' of independence cannot be hurried. For instance, if your baby is frustrated because she can't walk yet, calm her and distract her attention. She'll start to walk when her body is ready, not before.
- The most common reason parents give for not encouraging their child's independence is fear of injury – they frequently equate independence with risk. Keep her surroundings safe: always assume she will push herself as far as she can.

I can do it!

A 'can-do' toddler stands head and shoulders above the rest. He's the one who confidently approaches new challenges with great enthusiasm. Instead of thinking 'This is too difficult for me', he thinks 'I've got what it takes.'

I like myself

You can affect the way your child thinks about himself, and it's worth the effort. The can-do infant has a smile on his face because he enjoys life to the full. He takes many of the normal, everyday hurdles that could create anxiety – such as solving puzzle toys, learning new words, mixing with others – in his stride. The optimistic attitude of the can-do toddler shows through in everything he does throughout the day.

A can-do toddler's positive view of himself and his abilities has a number of psychological benefits. For a start, he is totally convinced that he can complete any challenge he faces – this makes him highly motivated to learn. As well as that, he likes himself as a person, which helps him to make new friends more easily. And his optimistic outlook usually encourages others in his company to be optimistic as well. His can-do attitude is contagious.

The 'can't-do' toddler

A 'can't-do' toddler expects to fail:

- His pessimistic thoughts make him afraid of anything new. Failure is the norm for this child and so he doesn't even try.
- His self-image is so vulnerable that he is easily upset by innocent teasing from you or an older sibling – he thinks these are thinly veiled threats and insults.
- He voices his feelings about himself and is quick to say 'Can't do it', when faced with any new experience.

Compared to the can-do toddler, this child experiences much less pleasure, is more tense and has fewer friends. Put like that, you can see the advantages of helping your infant to think positively about himself and his abilities. Fortunately, there is lots you can do to help him take an optimistic outlook on life.

Help me, please

You can actively encourage your child to think 'I can do it':

Make him feel special. You can boost his can-do attitude by taking an interest in everything he does, by letting him know how pleased you are with his progress and by spending time with him whenever you can.

Point out his strengths. Whenever his confidence sags because he thinks 'I wish I was better than this', remind him of all his positive characteristics – for instance, that you like being with him or that he helps you tidy his toys.

Give encouragement. As it's not easy for your toddler to persist with a toy when he thinks 'This is too hard for me', be prepared to egg him on. Your words of encouragement boost his confidence.

Respect your toddler. The challenge facing him may seem easy to you (because you are an adult with lots of experience), but it doesn't look that way to him. Listen to his self-doubts, take them seriously and then provide reassurance.

Suggest solutions. If possible, offer new ideas to your toddler when he is unsure what to do. It's not about you solving the problem for him: rather, it's about leading him to a solution he hadn't thought of before.

Praise effort, not just outcomes. Your toddler's can-do attitude strengthens when he thinks you are pleased with his effort, even though success eluded him. Establish a nurturing atmosphere so that he isn't afraid of failure.

New kid on the block

I'm new here

Nobody knows for sure what goes through your baby's mind the moment she is born. However, psychologists do know from detailed observation of newborn behaviour that her senses are already fired up and raring to go, and she has the necessary neurological and brain equipment to think. But what are her first thinking experiences?

Where am I?

The first thought is perhaps fleetingly about the strain of the birth. Since she comes out crying – or at least is encouraged to cry within a few seconds – then it is safe to assume she has some thoughts about pain. Although crying is an instinctive response, it is also a definite reaction to a physical experience. Hopefully, though, her concern with pain at this stage is for a few moments at most. Her 'Ouch, that hurts' feeling passes quickly and is soon forgotten in her excitement with her new surroundings.

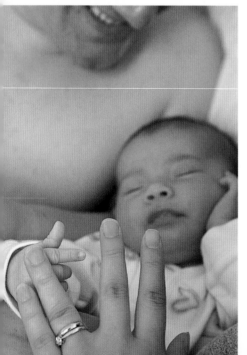

What's that?

The growing foetus can detect a very bright light that is directed to the mother's abdomen. Yet your baby's experiences of light in the womb do not match the bright lights of the outside world – there is still quite a contrast between the two environments.

Of course, your baby has no language to think with, but if she did her first thought at birth would probably be 'It's very bright!' Given that your baby has spent the full nine months of the pregnancy in the womb and is used to an environment that is dark, there is every reason to suppose that she is startled by the brightness of the lights of the birthing suite.

There is no doubt that your baby is truly fascinated by what she sees in these early moments after the birth. Many studies have examined the baby's reactions at that time and have concluded that she very quickly tries to connect with the adults who hold her – usually the mother, but often the father too. It is likely that your baby will be more alert for the first day immediately after her birth than she will be during any other 24-hour period in the next couple of months. Her thinking has definitely begun.

It's a bit chilly

Your baby probably also thinks about the change in temperature – the ambient 'room temperature' in the delivery room is likely to be cooler than the ambient 'womb temperature'. Added to that, she loses body heat comparatively fast when she is born: because her ratio of surface area to body volume is significantly higher than that of an older child, and because her layers of fat and skin are thin. All these factors combine to make her think 'It's cold in here.' These are two reasons why some mothers like to choose a method of delivery in which they are surrounded by darkness and warmth.

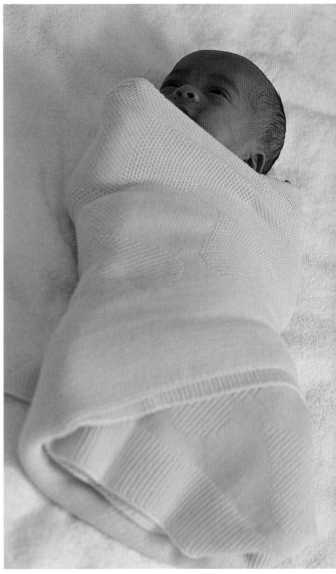

Hug me

Since your baby has been enveloped in the womb throughout the pregnancy, she may be unsettled by the sudden lack of 'touch' from you. Thoughts such as 'Where's my mother gone?' could be running through her mind. This adds importance to having warm, loving, physical contact with your baby as soon as you can after the delivery. Bear in mind that this is not about bonding (see pages 10–11) – there is plenty of time for that. Rather, this is about continuing to make her feel safe and secure through skin-to-skin contact with you.

I'm not completely helpless

Although your new arrival is totally dependent on you for survival, he is not entirely helpless when he is born. In fact, there are several things he can do physically without even thinking about them: for instance, he can swallow food, he can grip and he can blink.

I don't need to think!

Known as reflexes, these physical actions are inborn, involuntary responses over which your baby has no control. He doesn't need to think about these actions or learn how to make them – they happen automatically. The following survival reflexes protect your baby:

Breathing reflex Most basic of all, your baby constantly breathes air in and out of his lungs, and regulates the pace depending on his needs. This reflex stays with him throughout life.

Blink reflex If your baby sees a bright light or hears a sudden loud noise, he instinctively blinks his eyes. By moving his eyelids in this way, he protects his sensitive eyes from potential damage.

Sucking reflex As soon as a small object is placed in your baby's mouth, resting on his tongue, he starts to suck. He does this even when the object is not actually a food source, proving that this action is automatic.

Swallowing reflex Not only does your baby suck by reflex, he can also swallow food (and small objects) without being taught how to do this. Sucking and swallowing combine so that he is able to drink milk, and then later eat solids.

Rooting reflex Gently stroke the side of your new baby's cheek when he isn't looking at you. You'll find that he immediately turns his head so that his lips touch your finger. He instinctively starts to search for food in this way.

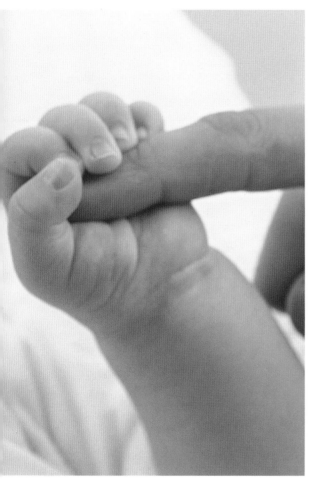

It's out of my control

Your new baby displays several other involuntary responses:

His feet are very ticklish. If you gently stroke the sole of his foot, he immediately fans then curls his toes. He does this every time – he can't help himself. Known as the Babinski reflex, this involuntary response normally disappears by the end of the first year.

He has a natural tendency to grab hold of things. This is called the palmar grasp reflex. Without attracting your baby's attention, softly place your index finger in the palm of his open hand. You'll find that he instinctively wraps his fingers tightly around yours and doesn't want to let go.

He has an innate desire to walk. Actual walking won't come until he reaches his second year, but in the meantime he has a stepping reflex. Hold your baby upright, gripping him firmly under his arms, then gradually lower his feet towards the floor. As soon as they touch the surface, he makes a stepping motion as if trying to walk.

He likes life best when he is upright. The Moro reflex operates when your baby thinks he is falling – he automatically throws out his arms and legs, curves his back, and then brings his arms together as though clutching on to an imaginary object to steady himself.

How long do reflexes last?

Some of these reflexes disappear in the first year of life as your baby grows (for instance, the rooting reflex, Moro reflex and palmar grasp reflex vanish between three and four months), while others are permanent (for instance, the blinking reflex, swallowing reflex and breathing reflex last throughout life).

I can see

Years ago, psychologists used to think that when a baby is born all she sees is a 'blooming, buzzing, confusion' – but research has proved the world is not a blur to her. For a start, she differentiates between light and dark. That's why she stares more closely when you stand with your back to a bright window.

What I see best

Your baby's eyes have special cells at the back that detect colours. These are present at birth and kick into action within a couple of months. Objects with complete contrast (that is, black against white) are the easiest for her to see, but she can also see bright, basic colours (such as red, yellow and blue). In addition, she has an inborn interest in faces: studies have shown that babies can tell the difference between a normal photo of a face and a mixed-up one.

Your baby has some distance vision. Estimates suggest that at birth she can see an object clearly 6 m (20 ft) away, that you can probably can see almost 200 m (215 yd) away. Her vision is pre-tuned to focus on a point 20–30 cm (8–12 in) away (see pages 10–11). The pupil reflex, present at birth, causes her pupils to shrink automatically when a bright light shines in her eye.

I'm watching you

These early visual skills help your baby understand the world around her, but she doesn't look passively. She thinks, and plans what to look at – your baby actively scans her environment, using 'tracking'. This is her ability to move her eyes deliberately in order to watch you as you move from one side of the room to another. She chooses to use her sight in this way.

Hold a small toy in your hand about 1 m (3 ft) from your baby's face, then gently move it around in a large, upright circular motion. From two to three months of age, her eyes are able to follow the object closely along its path. And by six months, she tracks an object that falls from her grasp.

How visual skills develop

During your baby's first two years, she develops other visual skills that affect the way she interprets the world around her:

Accommodation The lens of the eye varies in thickness in order to bring objects into focus. By the time your baby is three months old, her visual accommodation skills are almost as good as yours.

Saccades These small eye movements enable the eye to scan an object or search a general scene. Your new baby has limited saccadic ability, but this increases quickly during the first four months.

Vergence Normally, when looking at an object both your eyes move in the same direction, but when looking at, say, the tip of your nose your eyes need to rotate in opposite directions (vergence). Young babies don't have reliable vergence.

Give me lots to look at

Make sure that your baby's bedroom has stencils on the walls, patterned wallpaper in bright colours, or single-coloured walls with lots of different pictures on them. A low-hanging mobile above the crib will stimulate her visual searching skills. Your baby is more likely to be visually excited by toys in basic primary colours (such as red, blue and yellow). Choose picture books for her that have items displayed in bright colours, with a clear difference between the object in the foreground and the background.

I can hear

Nobody is precisely sure what your baby hears while he is inside the womb. Yet it is reasonable to assume that since sound does not travel clearly through fluid, any noises he picks up are likely to be muffled.

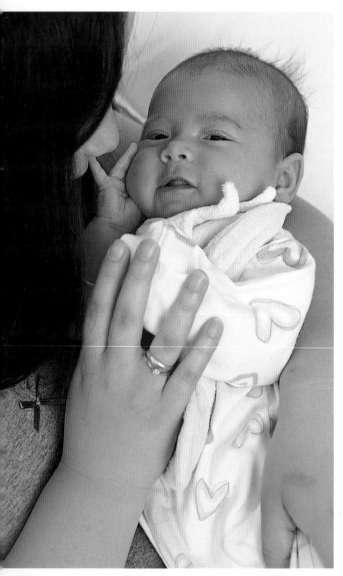

It's noisy out here!

Your baby probably hears sound patterns, such as loudness or quietness, sounds or silence, high tone or low tone. In addition, the outer ears of the foetus are covered with a thin layer of vernix, a creamy protective substance. All in all, sound inside the womb is detectable though unclear. So, one of the first thoughts going through your baby's mind as a newborn could be 'What on earth is all that noise?'

Electrical recordings of brain waves prove that a foetus can respond to sounds from as early as the 25th week following conception. Ultrasound images also reveal that when the foetus hears a sound from the 28th week onwards, he will almost certainly close his eyelids in response.

RESEARCH SHOWS

One study involved a group of pregnant women, each of whom made a tape recording of herself reading three children's stories. The psychologists then chose one of those stories, and the mother played only that story on the tape recorder several times a day from the sixth month of the pregnancy onwards. As soon as the baby was delivered, the researchers then played all three previously recorded stories to the newborn. The results were astonishing: the baby was unresponsive to the two unfamiliar stories but began sucking vigorously as soon as he heard the story that had been read to him during the pregnancy.

What's that you said?

Your new baby hears about as well as an adult who has a very heavy head cold. You can probably hear a whisper from a distance of about 1.5 m (5 ft), whereas from that distance he can only hear a voice at normal conversation volume. He can tell the difference between sounds of different lengths, different volumes, and even from different directions.

Sounds that have a low frequency are generally more soothing for your baby than sounds with a high frequency – in fact, high-pitched tones are more likely to make him cry. At six months, your infant recognizes his favourite tunes and reacts differently when these are changed.

I like your voice

Perhaps the most fascinating aspect of your baby's hearing during the early years is his ever-increasing interest in human speech – he is pre-programmed to attend to human voices despite hearing many different sounds every single day. Researchers have demonstrated that young infants generally prefer sounds that are of the same tone and frequency as that of normal human language. At less than four days old, your baby can tell the difference between your voice and the voice of a total stranger.

He can also distinguish between different speech sounds when he is quite young. For instance, when he is only a week old, your baby can tell the difference between the vowel sound 'a' and the vowel sound 'i', and when he is a couple of months old he can distinguish between consonant sounds such as 'ba' and 'la'. Since these small sound units (termed 'phonemes') are the foundation stones of spoken language, psychologists conclude that babies use their hearing very early on in life to get their language development off to a flying start.

I'm very sensitive

Your baby has around 10,000 taste buds in her mouth, which is a lot more than you've got! Whereas you now only have them on your tongue, she still has them on the sides and roof of her mouth. (Girls have more taste buds than boys.)

I'll just use my mouth

In subsequent years your baby's extra taste buds vanish and the remaining ones become less sensitive. In the meantime, however, her mouth is her preferred means of exploring and learning. You might even find she tries to cram her feet in there as well!

The ability to distinguish between a range of tastes is present early on. A new baby makes a different face when she tastes sweet, sour and bitter, so she can tell the difference. In addition, her facial expressions are the same as those you make in response to these tastes – for instance, she smiles at sweet and grimaces at sour. So she thinks about taste in the same way you do.

RESEARCH SHOWS

A series of studies looked at sensitivity to the smell of breast milk. Young babies were offered two breast pads, one that had been worn by their mother and one that was completely new and unused. The results showed that between two and four days old, babies cannot tell the difference between the two breast pads, but by five days old they start to respond more positively to the one already used by their mother – and from day six onwards they can actually differentiate between a pad used by their own mother and a pad used by someone else. As far as your baby is concerned, she thinks you are best of all.

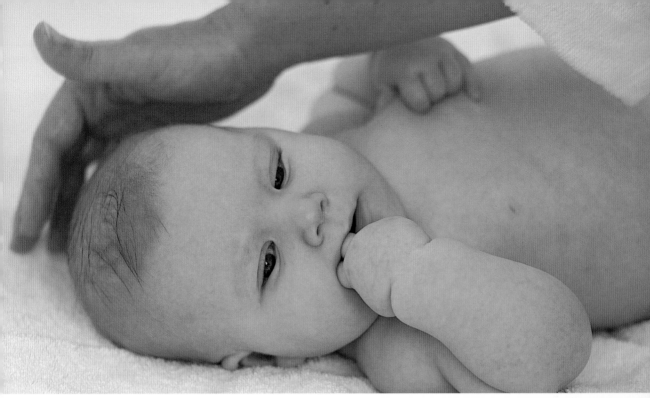

That feels good to me

Your baby's body starts to become sensitive to touch soon after conception, and by week 32 of the pregnancy all body parts respond to tactile stimulation. Her skin has around 50 touch receptors (that is, cells responsive to touch) in every square centimetre, amounting to about five million touch cells in total. There are over a hundred different types of receptor that pass signals to the brain about touch, pressure, pain and temperature, so when something or someone touches her she thinks 'I felt that.'

Your baby's sensitivity to touch develops rapidly within a few days of birth. For instance, soon after birth the typical newborn can distinguish the difference between the touch of brush hairs that are of different diameters; she is also sensitive to a puff of air that you might not even notice. And she certainly feels pain – that's why she bursts out crying when the doctor's needle pierces her skin to take a blood sample from her heel.

What a lovely smell

As with touch, your baby becomes increasingly sensitive to odours within a day or two of arriving in the world. She has clear preferences for particular smells. For instance, she has a pleased facial expression when she smells something fruity, while her expression when smelling something foul tells you that she thinks it is a disgusting odour. She is able to detect the smell of a wide range of foods including fish, butter and some types of fruit.

I like to move

You need only watch your newborn baby wriggling around in his cot, or in months to come watch your toddler exploring every corner of the house, to know that he's thinking 'Things look much more interesting over there.' He moves, wriggles, crawls and walks because that helps him to learn and discover. True, there's lots he can discover while staying rooted to the spot, but he prefers to be on the go.

I'll start from the top

Life for your growing baby would be so much simpler if he learned to move his head, hands, arms, feet and legs at the same time. But he doesn't. That's why, for instance, he wriggles his body furiously but can't coordinate his leg movements. He may jam himself against the side of the cot, and then burst into tears because he can't get himself out of that position.

I'm in control

Growth in movement and the control of movement follows two directions:

Cephalocaudal development This literally means 'from head to tail' and refers to the trend for growth to occur from the head downwards. During pregnancy, the head forms earlier than the spinal cord, which in turn forms earlier than the feet. And when your baby is born, he gains head and neck control before he gains back control; and he gains back control before he gains legs and feet control. Your baby turns his head from side to side before he can lift it from the mattress, and he sits up before he walks.

Proximodistal development This literally means 'from near to far' and refers to the trend for physical skills to grow from the centre outwards – the nearer to the centre of your baby's body, the quicker the growth pattern and the sooner he is able to control its movement. For instance, during pregnancy the heart and brain start to grow prior to the fingers and toes. Your baby can probably roll his body from side to side around the age of four months, yet will not be able to pick up a small object with his fingertips for another four months after that.

I'll do it my way

Not all babies, infants and toddlers gain movement control at exactly the same age. There is often variation in the way and time that each stage is achieved. Let your baby find his own way of expressing his innate desire to gain control over his body movements. Don't be alarmed if he doesn't follow exactly the same pattern of movement development as others his own age.

What affects physical development?

The fact that your baby wants to improve his movements doesn't mean he automatically achieves this. All aspects of physical development depend on a number of factors, including:

Diet and nutrition There is a clear link between food intake and growth rate. Your baby needs to eat varied and nutritious foods in order to stimulate his growth.

Culture and ethnic origin There are cultural and ethnic differences in growth rates. For instance, the average Australian toddler is taller than the average Asian toddler.

Genetic input The most accurate guide to a baby's eventual adult height is the height of his parents. The inherited genes play a part in physical growth.

Emotional stimulation If a baby or toddler doesn't feel loved, valued and cared for, his progress in movement skills and physical development can slow down.

Communicate with me

True, your new baby can't talk, but she thinks 'I want to communicate with you anyway.' She uses a range of sounds for this purpose. Aside from cries to tell you she wants to be fed or changed, or to go to sleep, she makes more gentle sounds when she wants you to know she is relaxed and settled.

How speech and language skills develop

In the early weeks and months, your baby has the following speech and language skills which enable her to communicate with you in her own way:

Consonant differentiation As young as one month, your baby responds differently to different single consonant sounds. For instance, if she hears the single sound 'b' repeatedly and then hears the single sound 'n', the change in her heart rate confirms that she knows it is a new sound.

Vowel differentiation Differences between vowels are harder to detect than consonant differences. For instance, the difference between 'i' and 'e' is not as clear as that between 'k' and 's'. Yet your young baby can distinguish one vowel from another.

Crying differentiation When your baby is only a few hours old, she reacts differently to a human cry than she does to a computer-generated cry – she becomes more upset by the human sound of distress. She's thinking 'I hear another person crying and it makes me feel sad.'

Intonation differentiation One study found that at the age of four or five days, a new baby distinguishes between words spoken to her in her own language and words spoken to her in a foreign language. This ability is probably based on the different stresses and intonation of each language.

So there is no doubt that your new arrival is able – and keen – to communicate with you, either by listening to the sounds you make, or by engaging you to listen to the meaningful sounds that she makes.

Talk to me

You can help your baby maintain her natural enthusiasm by making a specific point of chatting to her as you progress through your day together. Whenever she hears you speaking directly to her she thinks 'This is great fun.'

You might think a description of everyday chores is boring, but your baby doesn't. Every word you say, every phrase you use, sparks her enthusiasm for speech and language. Remember that the world is a brand-new place as far as she's concerned, and she is fascinated by all she hears. So you shouldn't be surprised when she giggles as you describe how you are drying the dishes, or stares at you with all her concentration while you explain that you are putting her socks on her feet one at a time. She just loves you talking to her.

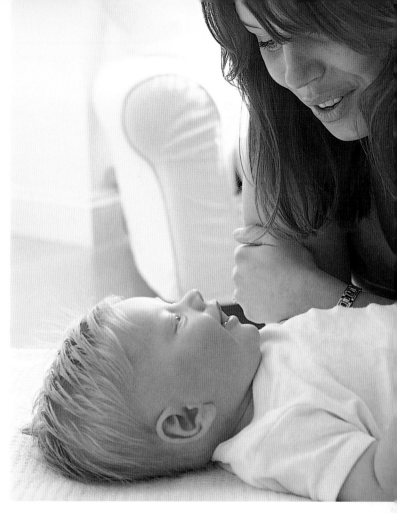

I'm 'chatting' to you

By the age of two months, your baby starts to make cooing sounds. These are noises that sound like words but don't actually correspond to any words you know or use. However, try to chat back to her as though you are having a conversation, because this technique lets her become familiar with the concept of turn-taking in language (see pages 96–97). Don't feel silly doing this: your positive response makes her feel that her attempts at speech are important. Bear in mind that she thrives with your attention, and even though she doesn't understand the precise meaning of everything you say, your baby makes sense of your words in her own way.

I know you

As you hold your new baby in your arms, you probably wonder if he knows you – if he can actually tell that it's you or if he would be just as happy to be held by any other loving adult. Don't worry: he does know who you are. When he stares into your eyes, he is definitely thinking 'Hello, it's good to see you again.'

How does your baby recognize you?

Your baby's recognition of you operates through a number of different dimensions:

Facial recognition A newborn baby stares for longer at his mother's face than he does at the face of a total stranger. So he can differentiate you from other people very early on in life, probably within a week of birth.

Body smell A breast-fed baby very quickly becomes sensitive to the smell of his own mother's breast milk (see pages 26–27), and it is likely that this extends to his mother's distinctive body smell as well.

Voice tone A newborn baby has a definite preference for, and recognition of, his mother's voice. This is hardly surprising, given that he has listened to it for the previous nine months. It makes him feel safe and secure.

Singing You might consider your singing voice to be dreadful and tuneless, but your new arrival doesn't – he likes it so much that if you make variations to his favourite tunes, you'll notice that he is less responsive.

Spend time with me

Within a week or so of birth, your baby is also probably able to tell the difference between you and your partner – assuming that you both spend a significant amount of time feeding him, changing him, bathing him, talking to him and holding him. Recognition occurs through familiarity – it is not automatic. A parent who wants their baby to think 'I know this person' needs to be actively involved with him, regularly, as part of his daily routine.

It's definitely you

It's easier for your baby to recognize you when he has several ways of using his senses. For instance, he's more likely to know it is you when he can hear your voice and see your face at the same time, or when you hold him in your arms as you look at him. He combines all these different bits of information before reaching the 'that's my mother' conclusion. Studies have also shown that the typical baby is more interested in looking at a face and voice combined rather than at either on its own, so look at him as you talk.

We're getting closer

This basic recognition of you improves to a more sophisticated level within a few months, enabling your baby not only to tell that it is you (as opposed to someone else) but also to detect changes in your mood, facial expression and voice tone. In other words, he knows you well enough to sense subtle changes. He begins to bond closely with you, responding even to tiny differences in your manner with him.

When a mother changes her lively facial expression while playing with her young baby (for instance, to look sad, happy or bland), the baby's own facial expression and heart rate changes with each change in the mother's facial expression and mood. A similar result is found when the mother alters her voice tone in the middle of an interaction.

Cry baby

Get over here, please

You may not be sure exactly what your baby is thinking when he cries – and much of the time babies seem to cry for no apparent reason – but you can be sure that when he does so he is generally thinking 'Get over here as quick as you can.'

My cries mean something

Your baby cries most frequently during the first three months, then his crying tails off. You may find that up to the age of six months, the worst time for crying is the early evening (see pages 38–39).

On average, babies cry for a total of around two hours every single day – some more, some less. Around 75 per cent of babies cry for 30 minutes at most before stopping: it just seems longer when you are listening to it! Crying is your baby's way of expressing his thoughts to you, because he can't use words to communicate his ideas and feelings. It's your baby's natural mode of communication.

When in doubt

Sometimes you won't have a clue what your baby is thinking when he cries. You'll run through every possibility and yet still be in the dark about the cause of his distress. Do your best to settle him anyway, despite the fact that you aren't absolutely sure what is running through his mind at that moment.

Read my body language

Non-verbal communication involves the use of facial expressions and hand, arm, foot and leg movements in specific patterns and combinations, each of which communicates its own special meaning. Psychologists claim that even when your infant can speak, in every communication of his thoughts to you over 55 per cent of the meaning is conveyed by body language.

You can learn to read your baby's body language associated with cries – it just takes a little practice. Here are some suggestions to help you know what he thinks when he cries (see also pages 38–39):

'I don't feel very good.' If in pain, his cry is sharp, almost like a shriek, then he gasps as he draws in breath, and then he shrieks again. And if the pain is associated with ill-health, you'll also notice that his limb movements are lethargic.

'I want you to keep me company.' When he feels a bit lonely and sorry for himself because he can't see you, your baby's cry is pitiful rather than loud, sounding as if he is sad, not angry. His arms and legs will not be moving very much.

'I want to be fed.' The cry stemming from hunger usually follows a repetitive sequence in which your baby cries urgently, pauses for an instant to catch his breath, then cries urgently again, then pauses for breath, and so on. His hands and arms move frantically.

'I need my nappy changed.' This type of cry typically starts off quietly because his discomfort builds up slowly, and then gradually gets louder and louder. You'll also notice that he wriggles about in his cot as he cries.

'I'm bored.' Because this cry is designed specifically to get your attention, it is more of a shout than a scream, as he tries to catch your attention. Mainly inactive, he moves his body suddenly when he thinks you are coming to him.

'I'm tired.' Tiredness makes your baby fractious. He whines irritably, perhaps falling asleep for a few seconds and then waking up with a start. You'll also find that he rubs his eyes with his hand or pulls at his ear.

Understand me

The best way to learn how to use your baby's non-verbal communication to understand what he thinks when he cries is to watch him in his normal daily routine. By paying close attention to his sounds and facial expressions, and matching these with actions you take to soothe him, you'll be surprised how quickly you become skilled at reading his body language accurately. (See also pages 130–131.)

I want to be soothed

Soothing your crying baby is not an exact science, largely because you often don't know the precise reason for her tears. Even when you do, and then take appropriate action, she may still remain unsettled. For instance, when you know she cries from hunger, naturally you feed her – but although that satisfies her basic need, she might have worked herself up into such a state that she starts crying again as soon as the feed finishes.

Help me settle

Here are some practical strategies that can help to soothe your crying baby. Remember to persist with one for a few days before switching to the next – eventually you'll find something that helps her settle:

Move her. Try rocking your baby gently in your arms, walking around the house while you hold her, or driving with her securely restrained in the car.

Give her loving physical contact. Try cuddling her close to you, carrying her against you, massaging her very gently, or swaddling her in a blanket.

Feed her. Try giving her an extra feed, a bottle of water, and/or changing her dummy (pacifier).

Provide background stimulation. Try a steady noise, such as a vacuum cleaner, singing a lullaby, or playing music quietly to her.

Give her a comforter. Try giving her a favourite cuddly toy or special blanket, offering her a dummy, or putting her in a warm bath.

React to her. Try distracting your baby's attention when she cries, reassuring her, or just holding her while you chat calmly to her.

Constant crying

Despite all your best efforts, your baby may be one of those who seem to cry all day, every day, without sleeping. These never-ending wails can be demoralizing. A crying baby turns night into day and day into night. Surveys indicate that between 15 and 20 per cent of parents seek professional help because of their crying baby.

I've got colic

The most frequent reason given for persistent baby crying – especially for regular evening crying in babies around the age of three months – is 'colic', even though there is no universally agreed definition of this condition. The term 'colic' derives from the Greek word *kolokos*, meaning 'to do with the colon', suggesting it is a gastric problem. Doctors use the term to describe a pain in the stomach that is assumed to be caused by a spasm in the tummy muscles. However, some crying at this age has nothing at all to do with pain.

In addition, the existence of colic is difficult to verify. Even so, many parents claim colic does exist. However, nobody as yet has been able to explain why some babies are affected by it and others are not, nor why the peak period of colicky crying is in the early evening, nor why it only occurs in the first few months of life. And there is no magic cure for this type of crying, although holding techniques and gentle massage may help.

If your baby cries persistently and refuses to sleep – whether or not she has colic – this could be one of the most difficult problems facing you. In many instances, it's as though the phase of evening crying has to take its natural course before it runs out. Remember that her crying is not your fault, nor is it hers. Resist any temptation to blame anyone for the situation.

Don't worry...

If you think you know what troubles your baby and yet your measures to settle her fail to have the desired effect. It's a case of learning through trial and error. The more you try to use your baby's non-verbal communication, the more adept you'll become. In the long run, this will enhance your relationship with her – she feels much safer and more secure when she thinks you can read her thoughts accurately.

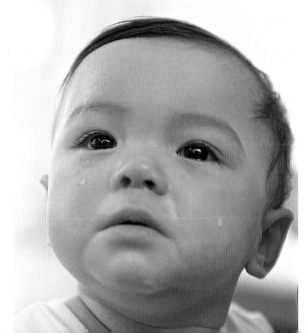

I like routines

Your baby or toddler may cry when his routine is broken. He howls because he thinks 'I like life the way it is and I don't want it to change.' And there are good reasons why he thinks this way.

Reasons why your child likes routine

Predictability Knowing that life follows a similar structure each day, your young child is able to anticipate what comes next – for instance, that bathtime comes after his evening feed, or that you play with him after he has been changed. Routine enables him to think ahead in his own way.

Similarity Your baby likes familiarity, stability and consistency. He likes to know that each day follows a similar pattern, so don't be surprised when he plays with the same toys or starts to smile when he sees you run the water for his bath. A similar routine each day helps your baby feel safe and secure.

Being in charge By the time he reaches the toddler stage, you will probably start to allow him to make some minor choices in his life, such as which video to watch, which songs to sing and which toys to play with. Having a routine with predictable activities that he can choose gives him a sense of control, which in turn boosts his confidence.

I'm unsettled

Just as routines make your toddler feel safe and secure, a change in routine can be unsettling and result in tears. He likes things the way they are and he doesn't want any change to this (unless, of course, he initiates the change himself). That's why you might find he explodes with rage when you suggest that today he will visit grandma instead of watching his favourite television programme. Toddlers can be very rigid in their expectations.

Tell me in advance

However, he can adapt to changes in routine, if you help him to think positively about them. Do your best to warn your toddler in advance. If you know there is an impending change in his routine this morning or this afternoon, tell him in plenty of time so that he can expect something different to occur. Help him to adjust his mindset by forewarning him.

You can build your child's flexibility and positive attitude towards routines by making a specific point of introducing small changes every so often. For instance, you might take him out instead of letting him play indoors as he usually does at a particular time; or you could suggest a different indoor activity instead of his usual routine; or you might give him a different seating position at mealtimes. Minor changes to his schedule help him to think 'I don't mind if things aren't exactly the same every day.'

I've got rhythm

Routines work best for your infant when they tie in with his natural rhythms. You'll already have noticed, say, that he is tired at fairly predictable times of the day (although this can change anyway every few months), that he gets grumpy at certain times of the day if he hasn't had a snack, and that he spontaneously settles down as night falls. It's as if these emotional states occur automatically, without prompting.

Your toddler's routine works best when it is in synchrony with these natural daily rhythms. Not only does he enjoy them for their own sake, but he also likes them because it confirms that you and he are in harmony. He thinks to himself 'My mother knows me so well.'

I'm sleepy

Your baby needs sleep to stay bright, alert and happy, and she may cry when she is sleepy. However, she doesn't always sleep precisely when you want her to. In the first few weeks, sleep patterns are typically unpredictable, though by the age of six to eight weeks her naps run more according to schedule and she begins to sleep for longer during the night.

It's dark outside

Some babies resist sleep at all costs, even when they are tired, while others settle down to sleep without any complaint whatsoever. Bear in mind that she needs to adjust to life outside the womb, where she was always surrounded by darkness; your baby gradually learns that the best time to sleep is at night.

RESEARCH SHOWS

A baby who is breast-fed is more likely to wake during the night than a baby who is bottle-fed, and a firstborn baby is more likely than any other child in the family to have sleep difficulties. This probably happens because a baby typically sleeps better when she follows a predictable routine; she thinks 'I feel ready to doze, and that's what you expect me to do now.' However, a breast-fed baby has more control over the feeding process (because she is generally fed on demand) and is therefore more used to setting the pace herself; and you are less experienced in establishing a routine with your firstborn. These factors combine to make an uninterrupted night's sleep less likely.

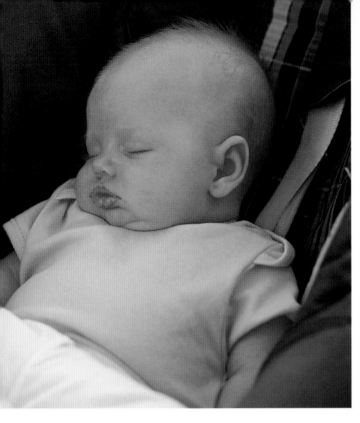

I like to sleep a lot

During the early months, your baby probably sleeps in total for about 19 hours every day, although she sleeps very lightly and at times you may not even notice that she is no longer awake. On average, she will fall asleep up to eight times each day. Once she is a year old, however, your baby needs less rest and she sleeps for only around 13 hours every day. Your own sleep pattern as an adult is quite different, so expect early parenthood to be tiring! But don't worry – her sleeping habits begin to match yours as her first year progresses.

Give me a comfortable room

Your baby needs to sleep, but her sleep environment matters. Sleep won't come to her unless she feels relaxed, warm and comfortable in her cot and wider surroundings.

Put her favourite cuddly toy beside her in the cot and let her have or hold her favourite soft blanket. These items help her relax by creating her sense of familiarity. She feels at ease in the bedroom when she can see and touch the things she knows. This means she nods off more easily instead of crying herself to sleep.

Background noise is important too. Of course, you don't need to tiptoe about the house when you are trying to lull your baby to sleep; on the other hand, having a television blaring loudly in the background won't help. Although your baby sleeps through most noises – and, in fact, continuous, monotonous noises (such as a vacuum cleaner) actually encourage her to feel sleepy – you should try to prevent loud, episodic sounds, such as your older children shouting at each other or doors banging throughout the house.

Dream, dream, dream

Your baby does dream! Watch him when he is asleep. You'll notice that at times his eyes move about rapidly under his closed eyelids, almost as though he is scanning a picture that only he can see. This phase of sleep – known as REM (rapid eye movement) sleep – occurs when your baby dreams. You may also find that he cries and whimpers occasionally while dreaming, or when he moves from one sleep stage to another; this doesn't mean that he's frightened, just that he's a little unsettled for the moment.

RESEARCH SHOWS

Your baby probably dreams more than you do. While adults typically dream for about 30 per cent of the time when they are asleep, babies typically dream for between 50 and 80 per cent of their sleeping time. Even an unborn baby has REM sleep while in the womb: ultrasonography has revealed that a foetus begins to have REM sleep as early as the 23rd week of pregnancy. Some research studies claim to have proved that between week 24 and week 30 of the pregnancy a foetus dreams every minute of sleep.

I dream a lot

Your new arrival dreams more in the first two weeks after birth than he does at any other time in his life. The amount of dreaming begins to diminish from that point onwards. By the age of 12 months, he dreams half as much as he did six months previously; and by three years he dreams half the amount that he did when he was 18 months old. By his third birthday, your infant's dreaming time is the same proportion as that of an adult.

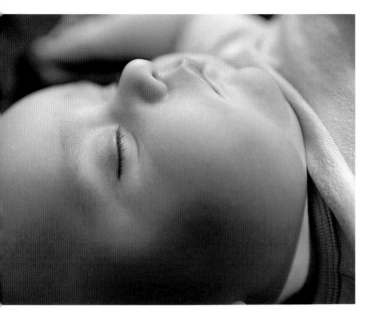

What a busy day I've had

Nobody can say for sure what a baby dreams about. You know how difficult it is to remember your own dreams – imagine how challenging it is for a baby to recollect his from the night before.

Yet psychologists think that one of the purposes of dreams is to help the dreamer reflect on his earlier experiences. So it is very likely that your baby dreams about what he sees and hears in the few hours before he falls asleep. He is bombarded with sights, sounds and sensations all day, every day. You take these for granted to the point that you no longer notice them, but your baby is more sensitive. He probably dreams about the sensory experiences arising from feeding, washing, changing and interacting with you.

I'm learning

Psychologists consider dreaming to be a time when your baby learns. To you, he lies there quietly with his eyes closed, resting, recharging his batteries for the next day's activities. While that's certainly true, the parts of the brain that are active during his dreaming suggest he is learning too. New connections between brain cells – vital to the development of his thinking skills – are formed while he dreams. It's almost as if he can concentrate better while dreaming than he can when he is awake because there are far fewer distractions.

Don't worry if you see his closed eyelids twitch very actively, accompanied by jerky arm and leg movements during REM sleep – it's perfectly normal. He is simply reacting to a very intense series of images that are running through his mind. You'll find that he settles back into a sleep rhythm quite quickly without waking up. All that has happened during these moments is that a new brain connection has been formed.

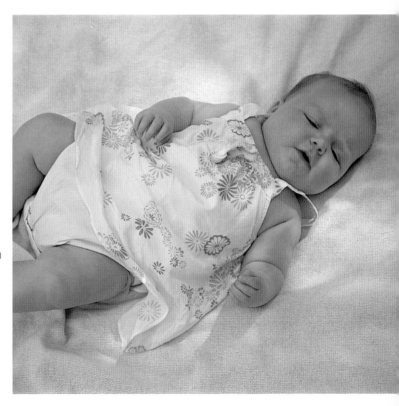

I want to stay awake

As far as your baby is concerned, life is very interesting and she'd much rather stay awake than go to sleep at night. No wonder, then, that she cries sometimes instead of sleeping – that's her way of telling you 'I want to stay up.'

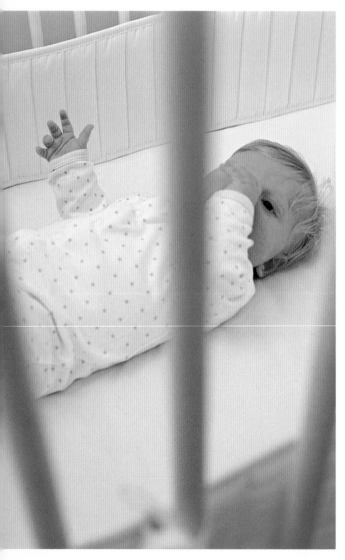

I can settle myself

By the time your baby is around three months old, she sleeps for about twice as long during the night as she does during the day – thankfully! For many parents, this is now a time when they can begin to predict that they'll have a good night's sleep without interruption.

However, your baby might be one who still protests at times, and who sometimes cries before she goes to sleep or occasionally wakes up screaming during the night. Give her a chance to manage this situation herself. She might be able to settle herself back to sleep without your intervention – after a few minutes, the crying stops and she gently returns to slumber. If that happens, there's no need for you to get involved; wait a few minutes before reacting.

RESEARCH SHOWS

Parents vary in their attitudes towards sleeping and crying. Some don't mind at all when their new baby cries before going to sleep, while others can't bear it. In most instances, a baby's sleep habits in the first four weeks are a reflection of her neurological, physical and psychological development and have little to do with the way she is managed by her parents (assuming, of course, that she is fed, changed and loved by them). Be realistic – few young babies go to sleep without complaint, the way we would like them to.

Let's party

There are two things to remember about your baby when she cries persistently during the night. First, she is a quick learner, and second, she likes to party. And from her point of view, the middle of the night is as good a time for play as any other hour. Your baby isn't the least bothered that the racket she makes might disturb her siblings, annoy her parents or irritate the neighbours – she revels in fun whenever she can find it!

Think very carefully about the way you respond to your baby's waking and night crying. If you rush in to her the moment she cries when she should be asleep, she quickly learns that this is a great way to grab your attention. And if you make the night-waking experience even more enjoyable for her by turning on the light, giving her a drink and playing with her, that simply increases the incentive for her to wake up crying.

Pay attention to me

There are ways to respond positively to your baby's night-time crying without turning the episode into a party. You can meet her emotional need for attention in a way that returns her to sleep, and yet doesn't encourage her to wake up in tears again the following night. For instance, you can go into her room, speak soothingly to her, perhaps even stroke her cheeks and hair gently, but without lifting her up or giving her something to eat or reading her a story. You could find that your presence in the room gives her all the reassurance she needs to enable her to return to sleep, and you won't be creating problems for yourself and her later.

I'm having a nightmare

Unfortunately, not all baby dreams are sweet. You may already have experience of watching your baby writhe and whine in the middle of a deep sleep, or perhaps even wake up suddenly screaming – he's having a bad dream: a nightmare.

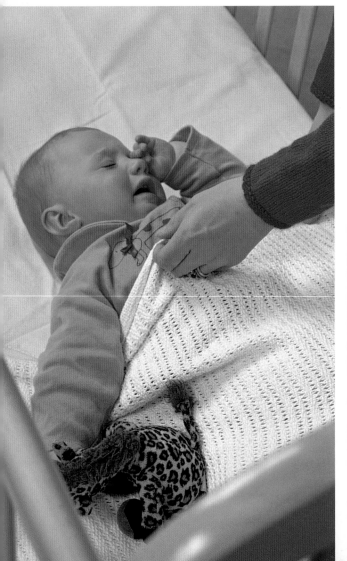

I can't tell you

It's very frightening for you to see him in the middle of the night scream the place down, with his eyes tightly shut and a terrified expression on his face. And the problem is that he is too young to be able to tell you what's going on inside his head at that moment. Don't worry – nightmares at this age are more common than you might expect, and the occasional bad dream during the first year of life is normal.

DID YOU KNOW?

Psychologists don't know for sure what triggers a bad dream in a baby. Possible causes include: a bad reaction to food or to a change in feeding patterns; a drop or rise in room temperature which makes him feel physically uncomfortable; a source of pain that arises from, say, sleeping in an awkward position; or unsettling background noise. Some evidence indicates that the tendency to have nightmares could be inherited. In most instances, however, the cause is unknown. Statistics suggest that baby girls and baby boys have nightmares with equal frequency.

Soothe me

If your baby does have a nightmare, don't try to wake him out of it as that could make him feel even more frightened. The chances are that he is not wide awake when he cries out – he could still be in the middle of the disturbing dream. Waking him up could upset him even more, especially if he thinks this is part of the dream, because it would make all his sensations more vivid.

Instead, reassure him. Once you realize he is having a nightmare, speak to him gently in a soothing, reassuring voice. Stroke his forehead or cheek softly. Although he is asleep, he'll be sensitive to these loving, physical contacts. Tell him quietly – but repeatedly – that he is fine, that everything is all right, and that you are with him to keep him safe. If your baby doesn't wake up from the effects of the nightmare, let him sleep on.

I'm awake

If you see that your baby is awake as a result of the bad dream, eyes wide open and babbling to you, he may have trouble distinguishing his dream from reality at that moment – he could be thinking that he is still in the nightmare. Your baby needs you to soothe and reassure him. However, never deliberately wake him during a nightmare.

You could also help him calm down by introducing a change of context: for instance, by lifting him up for a cuddle in another room, or by taking him downstairs with you for something to eat or drink. This sort of change of scenery makes your baby feel better because it introduces familiarity and normality into his waking state, breaks the tension and restores his emotional balance. Then put him back to bed. It is best not to keep him up for too long because he may lose his tiredness altogether.

Your baby may want you to stay with him until he falls asleep – that would be helpful for him, especially if he is still afraid. His immediate emotional need right there and then is for you to make him feel safe and secure.

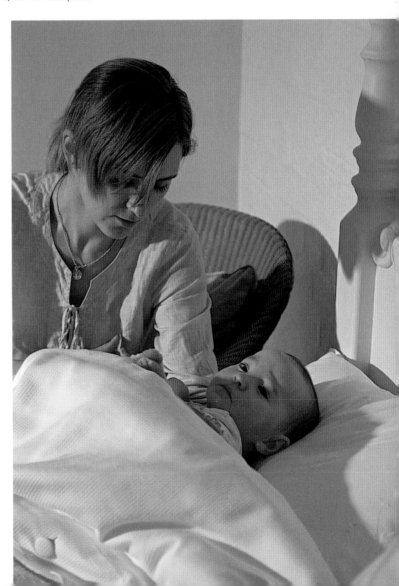

Little explorer

Up and at 'em

With so much going on around her, no wonder your infant is desperate to get on the move. The fact that her arm, leg and body movements are not fully under her control does not stop her basic need to satisfy her curiosity – the force of her spontaneous enthusiasm and innate zest for life far outstrip her physical abilities at this stage. As far as your baby is concerned, she thinks to herself 'There's a whole big world out there and I want to discover it.'

I'll make my own decisions

For the first four or five months of life at least, your baby only engages with objects and activities that grab her immediate attention. No matter how hard you wave that rattle in front of her face, for instance, she won't seek to learn about it unless her interest is triggered.

Sometimes it is hard to know why she is so interested in something. You may be surprised to find that your little explorer is attracted to the box the toy comes in rather than the toy itself. It's difficult to know what sparks her curiosity – maybe the colour of the box or the noise when it is opened and closed attracts her attention, or perhaps the texture of the packaging is intriguing.

By the age of six months, though, she is much more curious about the specific toys and games you provide for her. By then you'll be better attuned to her likes and dislikes, and you'll be able to buy new play items for her with much more confidence.

I didn't know this would happen!

Your baby is exactly like a scientist, except that she doesn't have any formal training in the subject! In her mind, there are no limits... at least until she comes up against them. In the meantime, however, nothing is beyond her realm of discovery. There may be occasions when, for instance, you respond to her screams only to discover that she has somehow managed to jam herself between the cot mattress and the side of the cot itself. And she cannot get herself out of the situation. She was probably trying to move in her own baby way towards something that attracted her interest, but her lack of knowledge and experience led her into getting stuck. Your reassuring cuddle is just what she needs to restore her confidence for the next round of exploration.

Emotional intelligence

As well as building up the part of the brain that deals with thinking and learning, these early explorations also teach your baby about emotions. The amygdala is an almond-shaped part of your child's forebrain which controls the development of emotions such as self-control, anger, frustration, fear and anxiety. Psychologists now believe that 'emotional intelligence' – in other words, a person's ability to control their emotions evenly, leading to personal happiness and mental wellbeing – is just as important for satisfactory development as ordinary intelligence. Since research confirms that the growth of the amygdala starts from birth onwards, your baby's emotional experiences during those early discovery episodes help her begin to learn control over her feelings.

The taste test

With so many taste buds, an ability to discriminate between a range of tastes, and an inquiring mind, your baby's mouth is an important tool for exploration. Yet he doesn't know the potential hazards of mouthing – his sense of danger doesn't begin to develop until much later, around the age of three or four years.

Everything goes straight in my mouth

So, your baby hasn't yet learned, for instance, that an item from the floor is likely to be dirty or that he could choke from swallowing small toys. Whereas you would be disgusted by a foul smell or taste, he is dominated by curiosity and he desperately mouths all that comes his way. To you, the object might seem brittle, hard and uninviting, but your baby thinks 'Mm, very interesting.'

One of the most convenient objects that a baby often likes to chew is his fingers. After all, they are always there, close to his mouth, and in a ready state for chewing. And they always have such a pleasant taste!

That feels better

The innate reflexes present at birth (see pages 20–21) mean that your baby has a number of automatic reactions to mouth stimulation including sucking, rooting, swallowing and gagging. As a result, he quickly learns that feeding not only satisfies hunger, it also makes him feel happy and secure. Once he forms that association in his mind, he tries to soothe himself by sucking things other than milk, such as his blanket. He might even start sucking on his teddy bear's ear. You may discover that this form of sucking occurs just before he drops off to sleep, as if it is a form of self-relaxation.

Ouch, it hurts!

Teething usually starts at around five or six months, though it can be a few months on either side. The first couple of teeth are typically on the bottom gum, with the upper teeth appearing a few months later. Your child has his full set of 20 teeth by the time he is three years old. Once the first tooth breaks through the gum, the rest usually follow at a steady, predictable rate of one per month.

Your infant drools more when teething. His discomfort can often be soothed by chewing on a hard object. Evidence suggests, however, that symptoms of teething are quite mild. Babies start to get a lot more infections around the time teething starts because that is when they lose their natural immunity, and this often leads parents to think, mistakenly, that their baby's fever is always linked to teething.

DID YOU KNOW?

The peak age for mouthing toys is between the ages of nine and 12 months, but your infant also tends to mouth objects more when he is teething because his gums are sore – and he especially prefers to chew on a teething ring that's fridge-chilled. He thinks 'That's hard and cold, just what I need.' But during teething he also thinks 'I'd rather chew on anything than nothing at all', so make sure toys that are mouthed regularly are kept clean.

Was that me?

Your new arrival constantly tries to interpret all the sounds, sights, tastes, smells and actions that occur in her world. At first, she has no real understanding of cause and effect, although psychologists claim that in the early days and weeks your baby does believe she controls everything.

I'm in control... I think

Think about it. When she is hungry, she cries... and food magically appears; when she is lonely, she cries... and somebody magically gives her attention; and when she is uncomfortable, she cries... and someone magically changes her nappy. While it is true that this is a type of cause-and-effect relationship, your baby doesn't grasp that the person reacting to her is not within her control. In other words, she is not actually causing the person to respond. That's why she gets frustrated on the occasions when her cries are not answered immediately – she thinks 'Why can't I get what I want now? It worked for me the last time.'

I made it happen

The earliest understanding of cause-and-effect relationships probably starts with her fingers. By the age of two or three months, you'll notice that your baby occasionally amuses herself by staring intently at her little digits while she wriggles them back and forth or fans them. She recognizes that they are her fingers, and that she can move them when she wants. The link between her ideas and her actions becomes established. She squeals with delight at these self-initiated finger games, because she is pleased at the thought that she has some control over items in her world.

This is also the stage when she begins to have the ability to shake a rattle with the deliberate intention of making a noise. Her increased hand control and finger grip, coupled with her enhanced thinking skills, mean that she deliberately causes the toy to move back and forth in order to make a noise. The look of pleasure is spread right across her face.

That's interesting

From the age of around six months, your growing, thinking infant is attracted to cause-and-effect toys (that is, ones that respond in a particular way as a result of a particular action). She likes the fact that she can choose to make something happen. For instance, she learns to hug tightly the toy dog that squeaks when pressed, and she learns to push the button in the activity centre attached to the side of her cot in order to make it ring.

As well as helping to develop her thinking and learning skills, these types of causes and effects boost her confidence; they reinforce her motivation to explore actively because they demonstrate that she has the power to influence toys and objects.

Try this

The typical infant between the age of nine and 12 months uses her increasing understanding of cause-and-effect for useful purposes. For instance, sit your baby in her high chair at the table. Put a piece of cloth on the table so that one corner of it is close to her hand while the other corner is well away from her. Now place a toy on the far end that is out of her reach. The chances are your little explorer will eventually realize that the way to get the toy is by pulling the cloth towards herself. That's proof that she sees the cause-and-effect links between her hand movement, the cloth and the toy.

Shake, rattle and roll

Your baby learns through play, and well-chosen toys can offer a whole new range of learning and fun opportunities for him. Remember that he has his individual preferences – there is no toy that suits every baby.

Now, this is really interesting

Your baby's vision tunes in most easily to basic colours such as red, blue, yellow and green. This means he will be drawn more to toys made in these colours. In addition, toys with lots of contrasting colours are also more likely to attract his attention and increase his motivation to explore. Aside from being colourful, toys can also be interesting to listen to (because, say, they make a noise, like a rattle, a music box, a squeaky doll), interesting to touch (because, say, they have different textures on each surface) and interesting to watch (because, say, they have reflective surfaces or sections that pop up). The more of his senses his toys appeal to, the better.

As your baby explores every toy through touch, but also through biting, chewing, licking, poking, hitting and rubbing, make sure they have no sharp sections, and no small removable bits that can be swallowed.

Don't push me

Your baby's thinking skills progress at a rapid rate. He likes toys that are matched to his stage of development. If you try to push him too hard, perhaps by buying him a toy that is designed for a much older child, he soon discovers it is too difficult and then gives up. On the other hand, if the toy is too easy then your growing infant quickly loses interest. The ones that suit him best are those that are slightly more demanding than his current toys but not so demanding that he gives up completely. Always look at a toy from your baby's point of view.

Are boys and girls different?

By the age of two or three years, boys and girls begin to have gender-specific preferences for toys. For instance, boys often start to prefer 'masculine-type' toys such as building materials, small toy soldiers and play tools, while girls often start to prefer 'feminine-type' toys such as dolls, dolls' houses and play crockery. There are individual differences, however, and you might discover, for instance, that your boy toddler likes playing with toys usually preferred by girls – that's perfectly normal.

There is much discussion among psychologists regarding the origin of these toy preferences, specifically whether they are innate or learned through parental guidance. While there is no clear evidence either way, gender differences in toy preferences probably arise from an interaction between 'nature' and 'nurture'.

I like stimulation

Favourite toys during your baby's first two years may include:

Building blocks because they allow him to explore and investigate, while at the same time improving his hand-eye coordination.

Story books because he likes to look at the pictures, point to them and listen to you read the story to him.

Inset boards because to succeed he has to visualize the shape, match it to his visual representation of the hole, and then manipulate the shape.

Nesting cubes because he has great fun fitting each of them neatly inside another, and this also stimulates his learning skills.

Crayons and paper because every child has some creative ability and he takes great pride in his achievements.

Too much information

The human brain develops in spurts: there are key times in life when it is especially ripe for growth, and early childhood is one of those periods. At birth, your baby has around 50 trillion synapses (communication channels between brain cells) and these double to 100 trillion by her first birthday.

My brain hurts

Stimulation, therefore, isn't just about keeping your baby occupied, it is also about promoting brain development. However, too much stimulation creates problems that can be avoided. It's as if her brain is pushed into overload, trying to handle too much information beyond its capacity, like a computer that suddenly 'crashes'.

The problem of over-stimulation

- Some researchers have claimed that too much television viewing for a baby can over-stimulate her brain so much that it causes permanent concentration difficulties.
- The type of television programmes that are more likely to cause over-stimulation are those that jump from scene to scene too quickly for a baby to follow.
- When a baby focuses on something for more than 15 seconds, she is less likely to be distracted by other things. This is known as 'attentional inertia'.
- Research has demonstrated that babies learn at a slower rate when they are tense and anxious than when they are relaxed.

I have to keep going

Despite her limitless energy, constant activity, and unquenchable thirst to explore and discover, your baby can become over-stimulated. The problem is that she is unable to regulate herself effectively.

Whereas an older child is usually able to say to herself 'I've had enough' when she feels too tired to continue, your baby just keeps on going. She doesn't know any better at this age. Unless you make the decision that she should end the activity now, she persists until tiredness or frustration overwhelms her and she is forced to give up. Her typical days should have a blend of rest, stimulation and interactions; you need to help her to achieve that balance because she can't do it on her own.

I can't cope

Signs that your baby's brain has been over-stimulated include:

Fractiousness Your baby starts to feel grumpy with too much noise and activity around her. She doesn't like to be bombarded with stimulation every moment of the day.

Poor concentration Your young baby has fluctuating concentration generally. Over-stimulation, however, reduces her concentration even further.

Passivity She doesn't reach out for the new toy you bring home for her. Instead, she just passively stares at it, showing no interest whatsoever.

Restlessness She becomes restless until you provide the next episode of stimulation, because she has already learned that she needs you to generate her enthusiasm.

Tiredness Plenty of rest time is needed between activities, otherwise she struggles to stay awake and her attention fades easily.

Unexpected tears Because she is so over-stimulated, she is easily upset and starts to cry at minor crises that she previously took in her stride.

Where's it gone?

When you put an object in your pocket or in a cupboard, you know it still exists even though you can't see it. Psychologists call this 'object permanence'. Your new baby, however, doesn't have object permanence – as far as he is concerned, he thinks 'If I can't see, it is no longer there.' That may be one reason why he cries when you leave him alone in his room: he thinks that you have vanished forever because he can't see you, hear you, smell you or touch you.

It just disappeared

Let's imagine that your young baby of around one or two months is attracted to a small toy because you wave it in front of him. Then let's further imagine that you drop the toy out of your hands while he still stares at it. You'll probably find that he makes no attempt to look for it – he does not move his head or his eyes to conduct a visual search. He thinks 'That's it, gone forever' and quickly turns his attention to something else.

At around the age of three months, there is a slight change in that your baby might at least continue to stare for a few seconds at the point where the toy was last seen, but that's about as far as he goes. Studies have demonstrated that if a baby this age reaches out his hands towards a small toy that has grabbed his attention, yet a screen is placed between him and the toy before he manages to grasp it, he gives up immediately and pulls back his hand. This is further proof that it is a case of 'out of sight, out of mind'.

I think I see something

Your baby's thought process steps up another gear between four and eight months. At this stage, he still thinks an object that is totally hidden has stopped existing altogether and therefore loses interest. But if he sees a very small part of the object jutting out from under, say, a cloth or curtain then he'll start to look puzzled and confused, as if to think 'That's a bit odd. What's that under the cover?' However, he probably won't reach for it.

If there is a larger piece of the item jutting out, though, he probably lifts the cloth to look at the whole object. In other words, he knows it's there from the fact that he can see a meaningful part of it. Even then, however, your baby's response depends on how the object became concealed in the first place. For instance, if he was actively involved (because he dropped the toy while holding it) then he is more likely to look for it than if you dropped the toy.

Out of sight, out of mind

Between eight and 12 months, your baby grasps the concept of object permanence. No longer a case of 'out of sight, out of mind', he knows that the object has simply been concealed and that it has not disappeared altogether. However, there are still some limitations in his thinking. For instance, he tends to search for a missing object where he found it the last time, not where he actually last saw it. It's only during the next year of life that full object permanence emerges.

Mirror, mirror…

The typical baby loves mirrors. They are exciting to her because they provide visual stimulation that constantly changes. One moment the image has a certain pattern and format, the next it changes in size and shape. She doesn't yet know that she is looking at herself – that comes a few months later.

What's that?

Your baby is totally fascinated by her own reflection or by the reflection of other people and objects. It all seems such a mystery to her, and yet she is drawn towards the mirror precisely because of her curiosity. She thinks it is such a great toy because of its ever-changing patterns.

Who's that?

By the age of three months, a baby knows the difference between a mirror image of a child and a real child. In one study, the three-month-old infants looked at the face of a real child their own age, and then at their own image in a mirror – each was presented to the infant alternately, in a fixed time sequence.

The first finding was that a baby this age consistently looks longer at her own image than she does at the live face of her peer. This clearly shows she can tell the difference between the two. Secondly, however, the infant's heart rate is much higher when looking at another child the same age than when staring at her own reflection, and she also vocalizes, squirms and reaches out more. She thinks 'I know this one is real and I'm excited about it.'

It's definitely me... perhaps

Your baby's understanding of mirror images develops significantly between her first and second birthdays. During this period, she eventually begins to realize that what she sees is her own reflection, that the image she stares at is directly related to herself – that's a major step forward in her powers of thought. This sea-change in her thinking takes place from around the age of 12–15 months onwards.

Try this

Psychologists test understanding of mirrors using the following technique. Let your young infant (aged between 12 and 24 months) play with a mirror for a few minutes (the type that is plastic and therefore safe). Encourage her to look at her own reflection. Then take the mirror away from her and put it to one side. Play another game with her for the next couple of minutes, and during that play time gently put a dab of red lipstick on the tip of her nose. (You have to do this so that your baby doesn't realize what you have done – you could, for instance, pretend that you are wiping a dirty mark off her nose.)

Once the red lipstick is in place, give her the mirror to look at again. If she fully understands the nature of mirror images, then she will realize that this is her face and that there is a red mark on her nose. Consequently, she will touch her nose on the exact spot of the lipstick mark. Psychologists have found that less than 50 per cent of children aged 18 months try to touch the mark. By the age of two years, however, almost three-quarters of the children try to touch the mark, and the figure rises to virtually 100 per cent by the age of three.

Again, again

Repetition is reassuring for your baby. He loves to experience the same things over and over again, whether it's the same song, poem, smile, toy or game. He seems to have an insatiable appetite for repetition.

DID YOU KNOW?

'I'll stick with this.' Most adults find repetition boring: for instance, you wouldn't want to see the same movie over and over again, nor would you want to hear the same song continually. You would quickly become bored and disinterested, preferring to move on to something newer.

Your baby has a different view. Repetition attracts his interest and enthusiasm; he thinks 'Great, my favourite toy again.' It's almost as though the more he knows a song, game or puzzle, the more he enjoys it.

This is familiar

Your baby likes repetition so much because he prefers the familiar to the unfamiliar. Despite his natural curiosity and desire to explore new places and objects, he has an underlying need for structure and predictability. And repetition brings that sense of security. He feels good with it.

There's something very reassuring about a familiar game, toy, video tape or nursery rhyme – your baby knows what to expect. Familiarity, in this instance, breeds a feeling of security not contempt. You only need to watch your baby's delight at these moments to realize that he gets a lot of emotional pleasure from repetition. He is not at all embarrassed or inhibited about going through the same experiences repeatedly; he assumes you feel the same way too.

I'm learning

This 'again and again' strategy is also your baby's natural way of improving his learning. When you try to learn something new – for instance, a particular telephone number – you commit it to memory by repeating it over and over again. Experience has taught you that this technique improves your recall, and you will continue to repeat the phone number until you are sure you can remember it easily. Repetition works just as well for your baby.

So, when your infant plays with the same toy over and over, he uses a learning technique that he knows is effective. He thinks 'Each time I play with this toy I find it easier to manage.' Repetition also boosts his confidence by guaranteeing him success every time he plays with the familiar toy or game. There is no better way to raise your baby's self-esteem.

That's too difficult

Repetition, however, can also turn into your baby's way of avoiding challenge and change. Playing over and over again with the same toy keeps your baby in his comfort zone, making sure he doesn't have to try too hard. There are times when he would rather not make the effort to move to the next developmental stage.

He copes better with the transition from repetition to a new experience if the two events are linked. Suppose, for instance, you want him to play with a new puzzle toy instead of the one that he can complete instantly. Let him start playing with the old toy and keep that beside him while you introduce the new toy. Stay with him while he explores it, talk to him enthusiastically and let him see that you are interested. Your involvement increases his motivation to try new things.

On the move

Can I hold it?

Reaching for something is much more difficult than you think. First, you have to fix the sought-after object in your vision and keep it there; then you have to move your hand specifically in the direction of that object, constantly matching your visual image with the movement messages coming from and going to your hand.

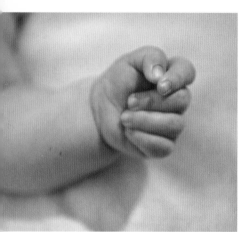

Oops – I missed!

Surprisingly, however, even your newborn baby can manage some type of reaching, although her hand-eye coordination is not very skilled. Psychologists call this 'pre-reaching'. As she moves her hand – often both hands together at this stage – she thinks 'Yes, I'm right at it', but in most instances she closes her hand to grip the object either much too soon before her hand has actually reached it, or too late after her hand has gone past it. Sometimes she doesn't even open her hand at all as she reaches.

For your newborn, reaching and grasping are two separate actions which are just too demanding for her to coordinate, even though she knows what she wants to achieve. She can't think clearly enough to integrate both skills effectively.

I'm getting better at this

By four months, things are looking up. Your infant's curiosity for the world around her means that she has not given up trying to reach and grasp objects – she is actually more determined than ever, spurred on by her increasing ability in this area. Now when she reaches, she thinks more carefully about it. She monitors and adjusts the progress of her hand and fingers as she moves them towards the object. When her hand veers off direction, she recognizes this and compensates accordingly by bringing it back to the proper path. However, reaching and grasping remain separate actions – you'll notice that around a second elapses between her hand arriving at the toy and her fingers grasping around it. She still tends to reach with both hands together.

I can do this now

From the age of five or six months on, reaching and grasping blend into one. Your infant's improving ability in hand-eye coordination allows her to think 'I want to have a look at that', and then to execute the reaching and grasping without as much concentration. It becomes more natural. Psychologists call this 'ballistic reaching'.

She also uses her whole body now to help achieve the target: for instance, by angling herself towards the desired object or actually crawling closer to it, thereby reducing the distance. You may even find that she leans so far that she actually falls over, crying with surprise at toppling because she concentrated so hard on reaching!

RESEARCH SHOWS

When your young baby reaches for an object, she does so through thoughtful choice and not simply as a random movement. In one study, each baby was given a set of special glass prisms to wear. These prisms tricked the baby into thinking that there was an object in front of her, when in fact it did not exist at all. The baby saw an illusion. The researchers noticed that after a while, each baby would reach for the fictitious object but would then burst into tears when she found it elusive. This reaction showed that the baby deliberately reached for the item. If it had been an accidental hand movement, she wouldn't have been bothered at all about not obtaining the object and so would not have cried.

I'm getting to grips with this

Your baby's hand grip develops in clear stages. First, at around four months, he uses the ulnar grasp (palm and fourth and fifth finger); then, at around five or six months, the palmar grasp (middle finger and centre of the palm); and then, at around seven or eight months, the radial grasp (index finger and side of the palm).

I'm in control

Your baby's improving hand grasp means that when he wants to inspect a toy, he passes it from one hand to other, in a deliberate manner, while he peers closely at it. The item usually rests in the centre of his palm, with his fingers wrapped tightly around it, allowing him to move the item in a way he wants, in order to satisfy his curiosity. This is a huge step forward in his development because it gives him control. He is no longer dependent on you to hold toys in front of his face – he can now do that himself if he wants to.

I need to use my thumb and forefinger

Your infant soon discovers, however, that there is more to exploration and discovery than simply grasping an object – because if it is very small, once he sweeps it into his grasp he can no longer see it.

Pincer grasp – the coordinated use of his thumb and the finger next to it like a pair of pliers – opens up whole new opportunities for your baby and begins to emerge from around nine months (although some children manage this at an earlier age). Now he picks up a small piece of food from a plate in front of him without too much difficulty. That's also why you need to make sure there are no small objects lying around: your baby tries to pick them up, put them in his mouth and swallow them.

I can do two things at once

From now on, your infant's improving hand grip makes life a lot easier for him. For instance, he acquires 'functional asymmetry': that is, he can hold an object in one hand while using his other hand for an altogether different purpose. He thinks 'I'll just keep holding on to the ball with this hand while building these blocks with my other hand' (especially if there is another infant around who might take the ball if he puts it down for a second).

Second, he makes choices about what to hold and what to let go. For instance, when he is about one year old, let him watch you bang two wooden bricks together. Then give him a brick in each hand and ask him to do the same as you did. He thinks about it, remembers your actions, and then copies you. The big smile on his face proves to you that he deliberately chose to use his hand grip in this way.

Try this

Thinking and planning about hand grip plays a bigger part in your infant's life once he reaches the toddler stage. He recognizes that he can use his hand grip in a variety of creative ways in order to solve problems. For instance, seat your toddler in his high chair, place a small toy outside his reach and leave a long stick lying beside him. After a few moment's deliberation, he thinks 'I can use the stick to get the toy' – he grabs hold of the stick with one hand and uses it to bring the small item within his grasp. Most toddlers between 18 and 24 months can solve this problem very quickly.

I want to sit up

From the moment you hold your newborn baby in an upright position, she wants to sit up. She learns very quickly that the world looks much more exciting when she is vertical, compared to her normal horizontal position. And for the next six months she pushes hard to be able to get into that sitting position and keep herself there.

DID YOU KNOW?

- Your baby's concentration is likely to improve because she spends more time playing with one toy while sitting upright than she typically did when she could only lie flat.
- Hand control also improves once she starts sitting because she spends more time picking up and putting down toys, placing them accurately around her.
- Other physical skills develop too, because she starts to lean to the side, not just forward, and even starts to pivot her body around without falling.
- You should discourage 'w' sitting (in which your baby sits on the back of her legs with her body bent forward) – this position impedes her balancing skills and leg muscle growth.

This is tough!

It's a hard struggle, though. Before the age of five or six months, your baby simply doesn't have the neurological, physical or muscular ability to achieve her target. In the first couple of months, her back strength is very poor and she flops forward if put in a sitting position – she can't do anything about it, even though she thinks 'I want to sit up.'

By three or four months, her back muscles are more mature and you can gently raise her to a sitting position by pulling on her hands. However, the chances are that once she's there, she still slumps forward.

Give me some help

Sitting becomes possible around the fifth or six month. That's when your baby can begin to prop herself in an upright sitting position, at least for a few seconds, before falling over. Don't worry that she cries as she topples – her dignity is dented, nothing else. You'll find that her tears stop as soon as she returns to sitting. Now that her muscles are strong enough, she just needs practice to improve her sitting skills. Her balance will gradually improve.

In the meantime, she might sit with one hand pressed against the floor to steady herself. She likes your help at this point, so that she can stay upright. Cushions spread around her will soften any fall and they also provide support if pushed close to her body. A cushion right at the base of her spine can give her the sitting control that she so desperately seeks.

I can sit up now

From six or seven months on, your baby's independent sitting skills steadily improve, much to her delight – she loves seeing the world from this angle. All the muscles needed to maintain a good sitting posture firm up, as does her sense of balance. She wants to sit for as long as she can, so you may need to make sure that she doesn't overdo it. At this stage she prefers to play with toys that are stable and static – ones with wheels that have the habit of moving away simply frustrate her. Keep gathering her toys around her so that she doesn't need to reach too far.

Why am I not moving forward?

Your baby's intuitive curiosity drives him to move to new places, to explore uncharted seas, to discover hidden treasures. And he knows he cannot do this by staying still. Within a few weeks of birth, you'll spot his first attempts to move forward. Your baby knows there is more excitement in another part of the room, and he puts all his energy into getting there – but he just can't move.

I can't seem to move yet

At three weeks, for instance, when lying face down, your baby can probably just lift up his head and no more. He might make a valiant attempt at propelling his body but he remains rooted to the spot. He probably thinks 'Why isn't the world coming closer to me?'

There are good reasons why his curiosity outstrips his movement skills in these early months. Aside from having under-developed muscles, and weak balance and coordination, the typical young baby has a lot of body bulk in relation to his overall length – for instance, a baby with a birth weight of 3.6 kg (8 lb) is, on average, only 50 cm (20 in) long. Relatively speaking, he has more fat and less muscle than he will have when he is older, his head is larger in proportion to the rest of his body, and his arms and legs are too short for his body size.

RESEARCH SHOWS

Crawling develops in stages – it's not a case of going from no crawling one day to full crawling the next. In fact, there are up to 14 different progressions an infant goes through before he can crawl effectively. Each successive stage motivates him to move on to the next.

This is hard work!

Shortly after your baby manages to sit up on his own, he also starts to crawl, usually at around seven months. With crawling, both sides of the body have to work together. He has to think hard in order to push his weight on to his hands, then move his arms forward, and then draw his knees under his tummy. And once he has done that, he has to do it all over again. In the early stages, sometimes he is baffled when he moves backwards instead of forwards, and he may become frustrated at these times.

I'l

You... that suit... in the wa... ldren co... ly wit... other bat... 3 them at the knee. He thinks 'This is working for me, so no problem.' Bottom-shuffling is quite common, in which the infant sits upright and wiggles his bottom so that he moves forward in the sitting position.

Not every baby crawls. Some go directly from the sitting stage to the walking stage, without any meaningful crawling in between. One study found that babies born in the warmer seasons of the year tend to crawl later than those born during the colder season, probably because at the time they start crawling they are wearing heavier, tighter winter clothes.

My first step

The stepping reflex is present at birth. If you hold your newborn under the arms and let her dangle, she instinctively moves her legs and feet as though she is stepping forward, especially if her feet are allowed to touch the ground. This is simply a reflex, which fades completely by the time she is two months old.

I'm on my feet

Amid the development of independent sitting and crawling, your baby's limbs are growing stronger all the time. By six months she can maintain a standing position with support. This advance in her movement skills gives her confidence a huge surge. Suddenly she thinks she can do what you do, what her siblings do, and she feels good about it. 'I'm on my own two feet', she tells herself.

Of course, she can't move out of that position or she falls over, and the same happens if you stop supporting her. Yet she has achieved the first stage in walking – weight bearing on her legs. From then on, it's only a matter of time before she achieves independent walking.

RESEARCH SHOWS

Walking is often delayed in infants who have sight problems, suggesting that a toddler uses visual cues, such as the spacing between furniture and the distance she is from obstacles, to enable her to move confidently and safely. An infant who doesn't have that information may feel vulnerable and be less likely to take her first step.

I may be cruising for a bruising

It is difficult to predict how the development from supported standing to walking will happen and at what age. The typical infant goes from supported standing to 'cruising': she pulls herself from sitting to standing (perhaps against an armchair) and then side-steps her way around the room, using her hands to support herself from one piece of furniture to the next, though she may lose balance.

She looks around, plans ahead and judges the space between two successive supporting structures. Sometimes she misjudges and falls on to her bottom because the second chair is just out of her reach. Undaunted, she pulls herself upright again and has another try. The big smile on her face tells you she is very pleased with herself. The world is opening up to her.

I can walk!

Your infant's first independent step forward, without any support, will typically occur at around 12–15 months, although many children don't walk until they are 18 months old and yet go on to develop normally. It's a combination of physical maturity, personal confidence and determination, and opportunity that makes her feel ready to try walking on her own. Attitude possibly plays a part too – an infant who has a laid-back approach to life may be in less of a hurry to learn to walk.

Your child initially walks very unsteadily, and is easily unbalanced. That's why children in this phase are called 'toddlers' – their legs are spaced well apart for balance and they literally toddle from side to side as they move forward.

Up, up and away!

Of all the directions that fascinate your child, going up is the one that excites him above all else. This is partly because the other directions are easier for him to get to: for instance, he can move sideways, front or back by crawling or bottom shuffling. Upstairs, on the other hand, is a huge challenge, and at this stage in his development he goes for the biggest obstacle course he can.

I want to go where you go

There is another reason why upstairs is so enticing – that's the part of his house where his older siblings and parents travel to with ease. He wants to be like them and to be able to do what they do. And the prospect of going upstairs triggers his curiosity because he can't quite see to the top until he gets there, so there could be a very interesting surprise waiting for him.

Fitting a stair-guard at the top and bottom of the stairs makes sense when there is an infant or toddler in the house.

I'm stuck

One of the advantages of crawling up is that your infant only looks ahead. He doesn't look behind as he moves from one stair to the next because it never occurs him to plan his return path. There are too many exciting opportunities up ahead for him to consider this, at least until he gets stuck.

Unless your growing infant is particularly confident, it is highly likely that he will reach a certain point on the stairs – probably around halfway, because that is when he starts to tire and suddenly realizes he still has a long way to climb to the top – when he thinks to himself 'I'd like to go back down now.' But the act of coming down stairs requires him to manoeuvre his body in the opposite direction, which makes him uncomfortable. He needs you to rescue him.

I need some support

Once your child is at the toddler stage, going upstairs is a skill he has to relearn. When he crawled upstairs, his body was tight to the floor; he could feel the safety of the solid step under his tummy. Now that he walks, he doesn't have that security. Your toddler's confidence increases with experience and success, although in the meantime he appears very shaky and uncertain – but determined all the same.

By 15–18 months he travels upstairs by putting one foot on the next stair and then bringing the other alongside it, while holding on to the wall, the banister or your hand. He has to concentrate hard during this activity.

What goes up must come down

The flipside of walking up is that your toddler must walk down. This is more demanding, because the force of gravity combined with his body weight makes him feel as if he is being pulled towards the bottom against his will. He thinks 'It seems very high now.' He may even walk up and then try to crawl down backwards, or he may just shuffle his bottom from one stair to the next lower one.

Your child needs time to build his confidence. Supervise whenever he is on the stairs, as this helps him both practically and emotionally. By 18–20 months he has mastered this skill and moves up and down stairs in an upright position.

I can do it too

Imitation is an important part of your baby's learning skills. Through imitation, she watches what you do, she keeps it in her memory and then she acts it out herself. And imitation starts early – with the newborn.

I want to do what you're doing

In one study, an adult modelled facial movements that a newborn baby can already do (for instance, the adult opened her mouth, stuck her tongue out and pouted her lips). Each baby watched the adult make these facial gestures. Researchers found that a newborn baby was likely to open her mouth more frequently when she saw the adult model open her mouth, would stick her tongue out more when she saw the adult model stick out her tongue, and so on. This proves that even at that age, your baby thinks 'I want to do what she's doing.'

We're having a conversation

This early ability to imitate parental actions provides important evidence that your baby learns through social interaction. Psychologists are convinced that these imitations don't occur by chance, that they are in fact deliberately used by her to engage your attention. It is assumed to be one of the earliest forms of social communication between you and your baby. After all, she can't talk to you using your words, and she can't move around the way you do – but she can open and close her mouth like you, and she does that in response to your gesture. She really is thinking hard about this, using imitation of movements as a specific way to connect with you.

RESEARCH SHOWS

Psychologists studying 'deferred imitation' – that is, when an infant imitates a piece of behaviour that she observed a couple of days previously – have found that this complex memory skill appears in babies as young as nine months. In an experiment, infants that age were shown three different toys they had never seen before. The first group of babies simply looked at the toys but didn't touch; the second group watched an adult touch the toys but didn't touch the toys themselves; and the last group watched the adult operate the toys properly but again didn't touch them.

The next day, they were all allowed to play with the toys. The researchers discovered that the babies in the last group (the ones who watched the adult play with the toys) were much more likely to play with them correctly than the infants in the other groups. In other words, at nine months they were able to observe an action, recall it a day or two later, and then imitate it themselves.

I'm learning by copying you

During the toddler stage, your child continues to learn through imitation. The emphasis of imitation, however, changes at that age. Studies have shown that whereas a younger baby uses imitation for the purposes of social communication or for gaining attention from an adult, a toddler uses imitation mainly in order to improve her independence and self-help skills. It has a practical purpose.

That's why you discover that your infant between 18 months and two years old is often actively engaged in pretend cleaning (after she has watched you clean) or pretend cooking (after she has watched you cook) or pretend teeth-brushing (after she has watched you brush your teeth). Her drive to manage without help is now very strong and she deliberately imitates your actions in order to learn how to do more for herself. She delights in her achievements.

I'm not afraid

A toddler knows no fear. He can barely walk, and yet he tries to everywhere as fast as he can without any thought of possible danger. Your one-year-old bashes into doors, walls, table corners, stairs – you name it, he somehow manages to bump into it – and temporary pain seems to have no deterrent effect.

Danger? What danger?

You've just told him to be more careful because he tripped while running too fast across the room, and then he does the exact same thing again with the exact same result. He is simply motivated by curiosity, by the desire to explore the unexplored, to discover the undiscovered – and this inquisitive instinct blinds him to the potential dangers that lie ahead. You must do your best to ensure that your home environment is toddler-proof.

Without any real sense of danger, your child plunges headlong from one potentially harmful situation into another even when he is not on the move. There are his curious little fingers, which he can't keep to himself. If he's not poking his finger into a hole in the skirting board, he's picking up grubby things from the floor (or small stones, earth or sand, if playing in the garden) and putting them straight into his mouth. He was upset when he touched a hot object, he cried when he didn't like the taste of something he picked up off the floor and he hurt himself when he bumped into a chair while running fast around the room – and yet none of these unpleasant incidents deters him from continuing with his devil-may-care attitude.

The reality is that your toddler has no real sense of danger: he lives for the moment and doesn't pause to think that accidents and injury can happen to him.

How do children understand risk?

- Children under the age of three years have virtually no ability to anticipate hazards, which means they need extra-vigilant supervision when they explore.
- Your toddler's judgement is affected by his emotions; even if your child is sensible and cautious, he may become totally reckless when upset or distressed.
- Excitement affects perception. The thrill of seeing his friend on the opposite side of the road blots out danger – he may try to dash right through the heavy traffic.

It's a boy thing

Research findings reveal gender differences in the way toddlers perceive danger. If your toddler is a boy, the chances are he will automatically blame someone else when he is injured accidentally (and hence be less likely to change his behaviour), whereas a girl is more likely to blame herself (and hence be more likely to change her behaviour). Boys generally think more recklessly than girls and take longer to acquire a sense of danger.

This attitude is perhaps inadvertently encouraged by parents. Studies have shown that parents are more tolerant of daredevil behaviour from their young sons than they are from their young daughters: it's as though they generally find dangerous behaviour more acceptable from boys than from girls. Very soon, the children start to think that way too. Unfortunately, when your toddler does hurt himself, the chances are that he forgets the unpleasant experience very quickly; the incident easily slips his mind, making him happy to repeat the dangerous experience the next time around, despite previous upsets.

Social animal

Notice me!

Your child wants – and needs – attention from the moment she is born. First and foremost, it's a matter of survival. Without adult attention, she wouldn't be able to feed herself, clean herself or stimulate herself, so instinctively she cries out, demanding that you take notice.

I want to feel loved

But it goes beyond the satisfaction of basic physical needs. Your baby also craves attention in order to satisfy her deep-rooted psychological needs, such to be loved, to feel emotionally secure and to feel valued. These basic needs drive your baby's thoughts and feelings right from the word go: she calls for your attention because she realizes that is the only way to make her feel comfortable and satisfied.

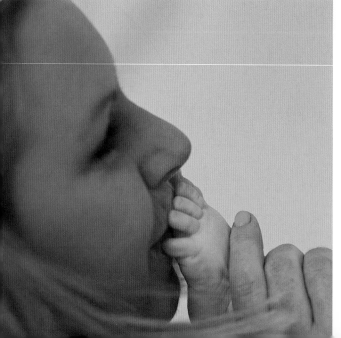

We need to bond

Bonding – that is, the close two-way emotional connection that forms between baby and parent during the early years (see pages 10–11) – is the platform for your child's psychological development. A satisfying emotional attachment between you and your baby provides the basis for her future relationships.

The only way she can form this psychological bond is by spending time with you, being comforted by you when she is distressed, being held lovingly by you, being stimulated by you and so on. In other words, your attention is absolutely necessary for the formation of an emotional attachment, and she knows it.

A child who has failed to form a secure emotional bond with at least one adult by the time she has reached the age of three or four years is likely to have relationship difficulties in later childhood and adulthood.

Negative attention

One of the infuriating characteristics of many toddlers, however, is not that they like parental attention and thrive on it, it's that they think 'Any form of attention is better than no attention at all.'

You may find that your one-year-old deliberately misbehaves, no matter how much you reprimand her, and that you don't have time for your own chores because you are too busy arguing with her. As far as you are concerned, negative attention (for instance, when a person is angry with you) is ghastly, but as far as your toddler is concerned, she may think that negative attention is better than being ignored – and that the more you berate her the better.

That's why ignoring a misbehaving one-year-old can sometimes be more effective than reprimanding her: this strategy makes her realize that she can't get negative attention by misbehaviour, she can only get positive attention by good behaviour.

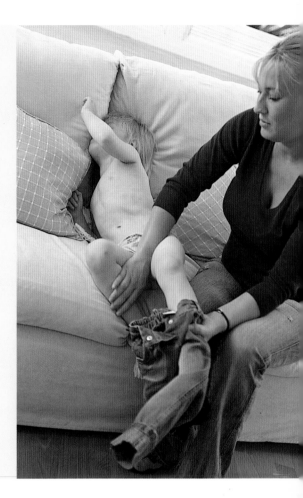

I feel good

As your baby progresses to the toddler stage, she continues to thrive on your attention, but not just because it satisfies basic emotional and physical needs. Now she thinks on a more sophisticated level. She knows, for instance, that your approval of her good behaviour makes her feel good about herself, and that she feels happy when you make a big fuss over one of her paintings.

In fact, your toddler's desire is so strong that if your positive attention is given to something she does (for instance, you give her a cuddle because she finished her meal without complaint) then the chances are that she will repeat that action the next time around. She thinks 'You made a lovely fuss of me the last time, so I'll do the same this time, too.'

Who are you?

From about the age of three or four months, your growing infant is fascinated by other babies, toddlers and children. If you hold your four-month-old baby in a sitting position on the floor, facing another baby the same age who is also propped up in a sitting position, they will stare at each other. Without any social inhibition whatsoever, you baby can't take his eyes off the other child. He thinks 'That looks very interesting.'

RESEARCH SHOWS

In one study, psychologists observed three-month-old babies and found that not only did an infant stare at his same-age partner, he would actually lean forward as if straining hard to get a closer look. Another study found that this curiosity about his peers is even stronger when his mother or father is present – maybe their presence boosts his confidence enough for him to be more socially adventurous.

I want to be alone

You might expect that this social curiosity would simply intensify as your baby grows older, but it doesn't exactly work out that way. True, he remains fascinated by his peers and seems to enjoy playing in the company of another child. However, he temporarily becomes more remote. It's almost as if he thinks 'I like him, but I'm worried what he is going to do.' This is known as the phase of 'solitary play'.

For most of the first year he plays alone, no matter how many other children his own age are beside him. And if another child approaches him – even if that child is friendly – your infant will stare and stare... and then he'll probably burst into tears, clinging to you for a reassuring cuddle.

I'm beside you

Another shift in fascination with other children comes at around 15–18 months. At this point, your toddler starts to engage in 'parallel play'. In this phase of development, his interest in his peers increases, though he is still not yet ready to play with them. You'll find that he now actively positions himself beside another child when the opportunity arises. Although you might expect them to interact, however, they don't; they just sit close to one another. The chances are that they will even try to copy each other's actions: for instance, if one tries to build some blocks the other might try this too.

But that's as far as it goes. Should one of the others have an abundance of confidence and break the social rules by coming in very close physical proximity, your child will start to draw away. At first he might only try to turn his body, though eventually he votes with his feet – by running over to you.

Let's get together

Your child's fascination with his peers leads him into the final phase of play, known as 'social play'. Occurring from around 21 months, social play takes place when your child moves beyond that passive watching stage and progresses to more active involvement. Now he wants to interact with others his own age through play.

The only slight problem is that his enthusiasm for social play outstrips his social skills and therefore petty squabbles often break out. Your toddler gradually learns that his peers have thoughts and feelings too, that they are not exactly the same as his, and that at times their desires might clash with his own. Through social play, your toddler turns his social curiosity into a social reality, helping him to get on with others.

Let's play

The only way your growing baby can learn social skills – that is, the various strategies needed for her to mix happily with other children – is through social experience. She won't learn how to share, take turns or be pleasant to other infants unless she has abundant opportunities to mix with them.

It isn't that easy

Until your child mixes with others she is used to being number one, the centre of attention. She is accustomed to having everything her own way, without considering anybody else. The picture changes when she plays with others, however. Perhaps for the first time she is made aware that her peers have feelings and ideas too.

Your growing infant learns a huge range of social skills this way, without any formal training: through trial-and-error, from other children's social behaviour, and from their reactions to her own social behaviour. Gradually, she adjusts and improves her social skills. She couldn't learn to play nicely by any other means.

I'm trying to control myself

Mixing with others also teaches your child how to regulate her emotions. During the early years she experiences a whole range of very intense feelings, including happiness, sadness, anxiety, frustration, dissatisfaction and anger. She learns some strategies for regulating her emotions from your support and encouragement, but she also learns emotional regulation from playing with her peers.

For instance, your toddler gradually realizes that when she storms off in a furious temper, the other children she plays with carry on as normal. Instead of getting her own way through rage or frustration, her peers continue with their play totally unaffected by her emotional expression. This lack of response from others helps her gain control over her feelings. Your toddler learns that her peers are happier to be with her when she stays calm and behaves positively towards them.

DID YOU KNOW?

Psychologists use the term 'scaffolding' to describe a typical learning experience in which a more capable child helps another child learn. It is given this name because once the learning has taken place, the learner is able to work on her own and the 'scaffold' of support is no longer needed.

Scaffolding occurs naturally in many play situations, because two young children playing together are rarely at the exact same level of thought and understanding, and the more mature learner instinctively encourages the other to improve her understanding. It's a form of peer coaching that takes place spontaneously when two children play together with a toy or game. Observations of toddlers confirm that scaffolding is a common phenomenon.

So that's how you do it

There is also learning that takes place from watching others play with toys. For instance, your child could be stuck with a shape sorter, not quite sure how to fit that awkward piece into the hole. No matter how much she tries, she can't achieve her goal. Then the child next to her picks up the toy that she has rejected and instantly puts the piece in the appropriate slot. 'So that's how you do it,' thinks your toddler.

Observational learning helps your child develop her understanding, her thinking skills and her problem-solving skills. Having the opportunity to watch other children her own age play with toys stretches her thought processes and opens up her mind to all sorts of new possibilities.

That's mine

Most infants and toddlers hate sharing. As you've discovered, your child desperately hangs on to his toys, games and sweets, to keep them all to himself. And he bursts out crying if any other child tries to touch them.

Hands off!

This reluctance to share is normal. Instead of thinking 'I'm willing to let her play with my toy because it will make her happy', your toddler thinks 'Hands off, that's mine' – his natural instinct is to protect his possessions at all costs.

Sharing is an important social skill that is necessary in order for two children to play together, but it only develops gradually. Until your toddler learns to share, he feels threatened and tearful whenever anyone else reaches for his treasured possessions.

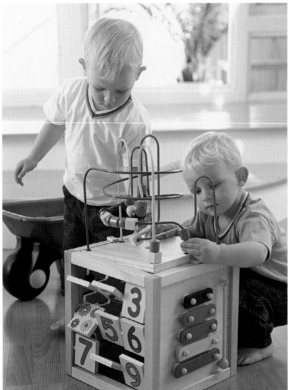

Think about this

When you think about what sharing actually involves for your toddler (and for everyone), it's hardly surprising that he is so upset about it. Basically, he thinks 'There's nothing in it for me', and becomes frantic with worry when another child approaches. Sharing requires challenging characteristics:

Empathy Your toddler has to understand the other child's point of view, and realize that his peers have feelings and thoughts just like him.

Giving Sharing involves giving something for nothing, because there is no immediate payback for the child who gives. He has to enjoy the simple act of giving.

Trust When a toddler shares, he has to trust that the other child will return the toy soon and in the same condition.

I can learn to share

Your toddler acquires the ability to share through observation, experience and teaching. Since it doesn't occur to him that sharing could have any positive value for him or that anyone in their right mind would want to share, he will only change his mind gradually. For instance, he watches you closely when you share out a packet of sweets, or when he sees you allow your partner to have the newspaper that you are reading. Observation of these practical examples of sharing makes him think 'So that's what sharing is all about.'

Eventually, with encouragement, your toddler takes that leap of faith and lets another child (usually an older sibling) play with one of his toys. Hearing you remind him that he will get his toy back boosts his confidence, and reassures him that sharing is safe. He likes to be reminded that the item will be returned to him and that he has nothing to fear.

I'm an only child

Sometimes an only child faces a greater challenge when it comes to sharing because, without any brothers or sisters, he is very used to having everything to himself. He hasn't grown up in a home atmosphere in which sharing was part and parcel of daily life; he may never have been asked to share before now. But it all depends on the individual child and his parents.

There is plenty of evidence that a toddler without siblings can be just as good at sharing as one who has brothers and sisters, if he is given enough alternative social experiences from which he can learn. For instance, he can learn to share by mixing with his peers at playgroup and pre-school, or when his same-age cousins come to visit. These non-sibling social experiences are just as valuable for your toddler when it comes to developing his ability to share.

Let's take turns

Researchers have found that newborn babies demonstrate good turn-taking skills with their parents. Through detailed analysis of close-up video tapes of mother-baby interactions during the first four months, psychologists discovered that a mother intuitively tunes in to her baby's period of attention and inattention, so that she very quickly begins to show more affection when her baby is attentive.

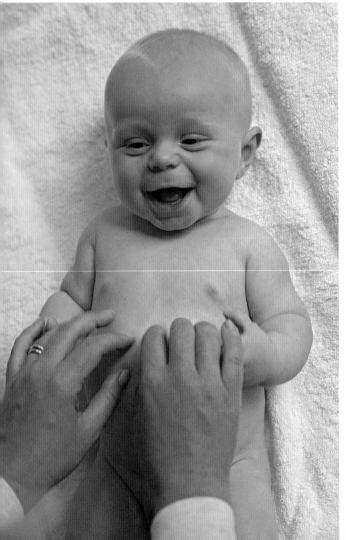

So this is a conversation

Once the pattern of 'interactional synchrony' has developed between mother and baby, a second phase takes place in which the mother waits for her baby to react in a certain way, then she responds positively, then the baby reacts to her response, and so on. This is an early form of turn-taking, which your baby clearly enjoys, and which proves she has the innate potential for turn-taking.

The next stage in turn-taking comes along as your toddler improves her language skills. When her speech and language really start to take off during her second year, your child begins to understand the social function of language – that it is not only to express her thoughts and feelings but is also a way of engaging someone else socially in a two-way interaction.

So having simple conversations with your toddler helps her become comfortable with the idea of turn-taking with language. She thinks 'I'll let you finish, then I'll take my turn.' Those routine chats that you have with her throughout the day provide natural opportunities for her to improve her turn-taking skills. Language games also help: for instance, singing a song where you sing most of the line but you let your toddler add the last word, or 'peek-a-boo' where you hide for a second or two and she waits patiently for you to reappear.

I can't wait – yet

When it comes to transferring this turn-taking ability into a social context with peers, however, things take a temporary downturn. Your child seems to forget everything she has learned about turn-taking so far, and instead experiences immense frustration when she has to wait – she thinks 'I want to be first and I can't wait.'

That's why she might kick up a tremendous fuss when, for instance, two other children at parent-and-toddler group are allowed to play with the toy ambulance before she is allowed to have it. Her only thought is probably 'I want it now', because she is still at the stage of development where she doesn't fully understand that her peers have feelings similar to her own. So she barges forcefully to the front of the queue, or pushes her hand deep in the bag of sweets without waiting to be asked, because as far as she is concerned turn-taking is for others, not for her.

The influence of others her own age is, however, very strong. As she approaches her second birthday, she begins to understand that many forms of play cannot take place without turn-taking. She sees that her own turn will come round eventually, if she is patient.

Turn-taking skills

The ability to take turns in all social contexts isn't established until a child is around three or four years old. Toddlers learn turn-taking more quickly when they use that social skill in the presence of a supervising adult – the knowledge that a grown-up is there to sort out any difficulties arising from one of the children not waiting to take a turn gives the young children confidence enough to continue happily with the game.

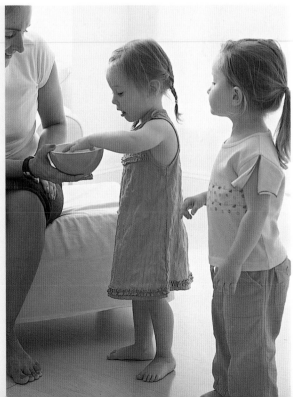

Don't leave me

As your baby grows, he has two conflicting psychological desires. First, he wants to become increasingly independent, to do more and more for himself without any help from you. Second, he wants to be close to you the moment anything goes slightly wrong, to be able to call on your reassuring presence whenever he feels the need.

I like you best

It is this second desire – to cling on to you during times of stress – that causes your child to burst into tears when you suggest leaving him with a babysitter or at pre-school. Perfectly happy until that specific moment of separation arrives, he howls hysterically at the prospect of your temporary departure. He thinks 'I prefer your company and I'm not ready to let you out of my sight.' He wants you to stay.

It's just a phase I'm going through

A toddler's anxiety at temporary separation from his parents is quite common. For instance, if he is left with a child-carer every morning, the chances are that he will settle there within a fortnight. Your toddler's clinginess when you leave him with, say, a babysitter, does not mean he'll have emotional difficulties later on – the two characteristics are usually unconnected. And even though he may be fully adjusted to staying with his current babysitter for an evening, he may be tearful and anxious when staying the next time with a new and unfamiliar sitter. One study even found that children who take time to settle with child-carers are more alert, more curious and more assertive with their peers, once they feel at ease.

That helps, thank you

Your toddler's tears on separating from you temporarily stem not only from his love for you. His distress also arises from fear of the unknown. He thinks 'What will happen to me when you go?' He is, therefore, much more able to cope with occasional time away from you when he knows what will happen during the separation. That's why it helps him to meet the babysitter in advance so that he has time to adjust to their personality and characteristics.

Likewise, he feels better about staying with a child-carer if he has already met them (and perhaps even played there in your presence a couple of days earlier). And if he is kept busy while you are away, so that he doesn't have time to reflect on your temporary absence, so much the better. Distracting his thoughts away from his anxiety and towards exciting play opportunities eases his distress.

Parent-toddler relationships

Psychologists have identified four forms of parent-toddler relationship, which affect the way a toddler separates from his parent:

Secure attachment The infant plays happily in the mother's presence, becomes anxious when she leaves, and greets her lovingly when she returns.

Resistant attachment The toddler stays very close to his mother, is reluctant to explore, and is upset when she leaves.

Avoidant attachment The infant is not distressed when his mother leaves, makes no effort to greet her when she returns, and does not mind whether a stranger looks after him.

Disorganized attachment The infant is confused and disorientated about his mother, and fluctuates between going towards her and moving away from her.

Secure attachment occurs in the majority of parent-baby relationships and is regarded as the best basis for a child to cope with temporary separations from his parent.

I'm feeling shy

When your baby is a few weeks old, she doesn't mind who handles her – she loves lots of attention, whoever it comes from. She isn't shy when strange faces peer into her cot in those early weeks. Of course, she is able to differentiate you from other people within a matter of days, but that doesn't stop her from enjoying the company of others.

DID YOU KNOW?

There is no single source of shyness:

- Evidence that shyness is genetically inherited from parents comes from studies which show that the levels of shyness of identical twins (who have almost identical genetic structures) are closer than the levels of shyness of non-identical twins (whose genetic structures are no more similar than any two siblings). However, this tendency could also be explained in terms of parental behaviour. Parents are more likely to expect their two children to behave the same if they look the same.
- A child is more likely to be shy or withdrawn in an environment that values competitiveness and attainments, rather than valuing a child for his personal qualities.
- Before the age of five years, boys tend to have a higher level of shyness than girls, but this trend reverses once the children attend school.

Who are you?

This openness with strangers typically vanishes around the age of six months. Instead of fascination and pleasure at unfamiliar faces, your six-month-old infant now bursts into tears the moment a strange child or adult enters her line of vision. Because she is more aware of her surroundings at this age, she thinks 'I don't know that person and I'm nervous', and so she is more likely to experience shyness.

I keep changing

Your child's shyness fluctuates during her first two years, often depending on the specific context in which she meets the other person: for instance, in the supermarket (she can be relaxed until someone she hasn't met before stops to talk to her, then her little face crumples with shyness) or at family gatherings (when you show off your lovely infant to a distant relative, she bursts out crying in response).

Her shyness with unfamiliar people changes regularly during this first year. One month she may be distraught at the sight of someone else and yet the following month she might be comfortable in the company of a stranger. Fortunately, these episodes are only temporary and she soon settles down as her confidence increases.

I need your help

When your toddler has an episode of shyness, her instinct is to remove herself as quickly as possible from the social situation, perhaps by turning her body away from the speaker, running out of the room or burying her face against you. She thinks 'I want out of here.' But the problem with this strategy is that when the next bout of shyness comes along, your toddler feels even less confident socially and makes an even bigger effort to run away as fast as she can.

In contrast, your gentle persuasion and encouragement to stay where she is, to face the child or adult of whom she is shy, makes her think 'That's not so bad after all.' She learns how to cope more effectively with her shyness as a result of your support at these times. She feels proud of her achievement and is more robust socially. As she overcomes successive episodes of shyness, your toddler feels increasingly good about herself.

I like to laugh

Your baby usually shows his first real smile when he is around six weeks old. Many parents say that their baby smiles earlier than this, but psychologists believe these earlier 'smiles' are simply facial expression, nothing more.

RESEARCH SHOWS

Toddlers are usually more attentive to a short story read to them when it contains an element of humour, and this can be a positive way to gain their interest and attention. Boys tend to recognize and respond to visual humour more easily than girls – when young boys and girls are shown cartoons, silly drawings, or even an amusing slapstick scenario involving a clown, boys usually laugh sooner than girls – and boys' humour tends to be at the expense of others.

Now that's what I call funny

Your infant's sense of humour changes as he changes:

Three months He chuckles at a familiar, friendly touch (for instance, when you nuzzle your face gently against his tummy and blow slowly on his skin).

Six months His humour and laughter is triggered by active movements (for instance, when you tickle him gently under his arms, or up and down his sides).

Nine months Unusual situations often stimulate his laughter (for instance, when you put his favourite teddy bear up your jumper so that only the head pokes out, and then ask 'Where's teddy?').

One year The focus of humour shifts away from himself towards objects and people in his environment (for instance, when you play peek-a-boo with him by hiding your face behind your cupped hands, then peering out from behind them). He squeaks with delight.

Two years Your toddler laughs most at humour that involves arm, leg and whole-body movement (for instance, when you play action rhymes such as Ring-a-ring-o'-roses).

The importance of laughter

There are a number of reasons why humour and laughter are important for your child's satisfactory emotional development:

■ Humour is a shared experience which brings you closer together. The focus of the humour doesn't matter: what does matter is that you and your child are relaxed and in tune with each other's happiness.

■ Your toddler can use humour to release tension – so he might laugh when he is reprimanded, not because he finds it funny but because the reprimand makes him feel nervous.

■ Humour and laughter are your child's instinctive ways of expressing his happiness. Of course, he laughs at a funny joke. Laughter is a universal expression of pleasure, across all cultures.

You can't *make* me laugh

Laughter is such an individual response that you can never really be sure what will stimulate your infant's humour.

Humour is often funniest when it occurs spontaneously, not when it is contrived. Relax when you are with your toddler and you'll find that laughter arises without any effort. Just be yourself. You'll find that you laugh lots when you are together because he thinks 'You're laughing so I'll laugh.' Your young child likes humour to be explicit, obvious and exaggerated: for instance, someone almost getting a 'custard pie' in the face isn't nearly as funny as them really getting it in the face. The visual image amuses him.

On the other hand, your toddler might be one of those children with a stone-faced expression who never seems to laugh at anything – a sense of humour is simply one personality trait and, like all human characteristics, it varies from child to child. Some children laugh more than others, that's all.

True self

That's annoying me

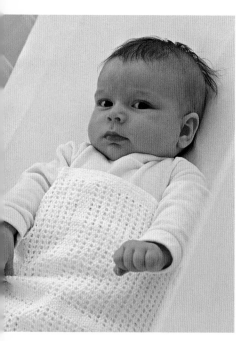

When you look around at other young babies and toddlers, you'll notice some are easier to manage than others. Yours might be one of those who goes with the flow, who copes with life's little changes and minor upsets without making a fuss – or she might be one who is very irritable and who thinks 'Everything annoys me.'

It's just how I am

A baby starts to show her temperament the moment she is born. For instance, maybe she sucks well and enthusiastically during her first feed or maybe she seems passive and only sucks slowly. Perhaps she lies calmly in the cot when nobody is directly involved with her, or she may move about a lot in order to get attention. Similarly, some babies are very settled and easy to manage while others are fractious, restless and difficult to calm.

RESEARCH SHOWS

Identical twins are more likely to have a similar temperament than non-identical twins, which strongly suggests your baby inherits part of her temperament profile from you and your partner. Further evidence for this comes from investigations into ethnic differences. One project found that babies from the USA are more anxious and moody than those from Ireland, who are in turn more active and restless than babies born in China. Yet the environment also plays a part. For instance, research has found that the more parents show positive affection towards their baby, the more likely she is to be sociable, happy and smiling herself. Your home environment can shape your baby's temperament.

What am I like?

Your infant's temperament probably falls into one of three types. (You may find, however, that she shares features from more than one type – this occurs in approximately one-quarter of all children.)

Easy The easy baby is a pleasure to be with because she is even-tempered and responds positively to anything that happens to her or around her. She adapts to new experiences, welcoming them rather than avoiding them. Her mood and behaviour is regular and predictable. She thinks 'I like life.'

Difficult The difficult baby is active for most of the time but is fractious and easily irritated. It doesn't take much to unsettle her; her moods vary and are unpredictable. This type of baby dislikes change and struggles to adapt to new situations or unfamiliar faces. She thinks 'Life irritates me.'

Slow to warm up The slow-to-warm up baby has mild reactions to most things. Lacking enthusiasm for new experiences, her responses are casual. For instance, if she doesn't like a new toy she will simply turn her head away from it rather than physically reject it. She thinks 'I want to take life easy.'

The five main components of temperament

Activity level Your baby's might be quick and energetic or she may be relaxed and sluggish, content to respond at her own steady pace.

Irritability Some babies and toddlers cope with everyday experiences without becoming rattled while others are easily irritated or upset.

Soothability This refers to the ease with which she calms down after she is upset, and varies greatly from child to child.

Fearfulness Stimulation can generate excitement or fear, and some babies and toddlers are more easily frightened than others.

Sociability The sociable child's lovely smile when someone approaches is much more pleasing than the howls of anxiety from an unsociable toddler.

I'll do it my way

Your baby's temperament is the foundation stone on which his later personality is built, and this emerges during the toddler and childhood years. These long-lasting characteristics affect the way he relates to other children and adults.

DID YOU KNOW?

Every baby has his own mixture of personal traits that make him unique. When he sees another baby or toddler behave in a certain way, he finds that fascinating but thinks 'No, I'm going to do it my way' – he has his own personality and style of doing things.

What is personality?

Psychologists claim that every child's personality is a blend of five different descriptive features:

Outgoing The extent to which he actively seeks the company of others so that he can play with them.

Agreeable The extent to which he is warm and compassionate to his peers, rather than being antagonistic.

Conscientious The extent to which he controls his impulses because he is aware of the needs of others.

Unstable The extent to which he finds everyday routine experiences threatening, upsetting or frightening.

Open The extent to which he is open to new experiences, plus his ability to be imaginative and creative.

Are girls and boys different?

There are gender differences in personality. For instance:

- Although toddlers of both genders often wear the same type of clothes (sweatshirt, jogging pants, trainers), more girls than boys wear clothes that are pink – boys tend to prefer darker colours.
- Boys usually prefer outdoor play while girls generally like more sedate activities.
- Boys are more likely than girls to hit and kick each other when they disagree; when girls bicker they are more likely to use words.
- Girls achieve independence at an earlier age than boys, and are quicker at learning how to dress and undress themselves and how to manage bowel and bladder control independently.
- Boys tend to be more adventurous than girls; they are more likely to take risks.
- Girls are quicker at learning how to co-operate with each other – they think 'We play better when we get on with each other.' That's why young girls are often able to play quietly together in games, while boys of the same age are more likely to squabble with each other.

I'm the first

Your child's birth order (that is, firstborn, secondborn, middle or youngest) affects his personality. For instance, firstborn children tend to be the brightest in the family and to achieve most, yet they are more likely to lack confidence and have high anxiety. They also tend to be more conformist, more responsible, and to enjoy traditional toys and games.

Your firstborn is in the unique position of being an only child for a couple of years and enjoys being the centre of attention during this period. However, he then has to cope with the trauma of a newborn baby in the family – and he may think 'Who is this, pushing me out of the limelight?'

This is the point when sibling rivalry usually begins – it's hardly surprising your firstborn is concerned about having to share you with another baby. The chances are, though, that he'll adjust happily within a few months, if you use sensitive strategies: for instance, giving your firstborn lots of attention too, involving him in some way with the practical care of the new baby, and emphasizing how much his little sibling adores him and looks up to him.

I am who I am

Right from birth, your baby has some sense that she is separate from you, and this 'sense of self' continues to grow during her first years. For instance, she is delighted when she shakes the rattle to make a noise because she thinks 'It was me who made that happen', and her sense of self grows. She also gradually learns that she can be happy on her own, and isn't totally dependent on others all the time.

There's no one else like me

The next stage is when your toddler begins to recognize that not only is she is a separate individual, but she also has certain characteristics, such as size, colour, gender, name and personality, just like any other object or being in the world. This genuine self-awareness usually begins to emerge when she is between 15 and 18 months old.

That's one of the reasons why mirror play (see pages 64–65) is so popular at this age – your toddler delights in seeing her own reflection. She thinks 'That's me there'. Through looking at her mirror image, and also at video clips and photos of herself, she continues to build her feeling of uniqueness.

I want you to like me

Aside from becoming self-willed – your toddler insists on doing things by herself – her increasing sense of self also causes her to be much more self-aware. Previously she did exactly what she wanted without a thought for anyone else; now, she starts to experience feelings such as pride, embarrassment and shyness.

These emotions arise from around the age of two years because your toddler starts to think 'Other people have an opinion about me.' She wants people to think highly of her, and she is disappointed when this doesn't happen.

How gender awareness develops

Your child's awareness of gender develops over time, until eventually she thinks 'I'm a girl!'

Three months Your baby can tell the difference between a man's face and a woman's. If she sees several photos of women she loses interest, but becomes attentive again when the sequence suddenly contains a photo of a man.

Six months In one research project, babies were shown a photo and heard a voice talking at the same time. The researchers found that a baby looked longer at the picture when the gender of the voice matched the gender of the person in the photo.

One year An infant's sense of gender is developing. For instance, if a girl this age mixes with toddlers wearing unisex clothing she will tend to stay beside the girls (and a boy will tend to stay beside the boys).

Two years Gender preferences for toys emerge. For instance, most girls prefer dolls and imaginative play, while most boys like toy cars and rough-and-tumble play.

I can take charge

Self-control is part of self-awareness. Despite all the temptations to do exactly as she pleases, your toddler will begin to correct herself. For instance, she might reach for an ornament that she knows she shouldn't touch while saying loudly to herself 'No, no, no' – this is her attempt to regulate her own behaviour.

She also gives herself instructions: for instance, while trying to put a toy into the toy box, she says loudly 'Put it in, put it in.' Known as 'self-directed speech', this is your toddler's way of controlling and regulating her own actions. By the time she is three years old, she thinks these thoughts instead of actually voicing them.

Me, me, me

When your toddler wants a toy to play with, for instance, he expects to get it right away. He isn't bothered by the fact that you are tired, or that his pal is already playing with it, or that you've already told him he can't play with it until later.

I'm the most important

As far as your egocentric toddler is concerned, he comes first and other people's thoughts and feelings don't matter. His main thought is 'Me, myself, I; what I want I must have.' And if you have the cheek to stand in his way, he may erupt with temper. It's almost as if he is outraged by your impertinence at not doing what he wants, when he wants you to! The determination of your furious egocentric toddler knows no limits; he pushes hard to get what he wants.

I'm not selfish

If you behaved this way, people would say you were selfish because you would be making a conscious choice to ignore other people's feelings in order to suit yourself; you would deliberately be putting your own feelings ahead of others'.

However, you can't describe the same behaviour in your toddler as selfish because he doesn't have your level of understanding – rather, his behaviour is 'egocentric' in the true sense of the word, instead of 'selfish' in the adult sense of the word. Your toddler is egocentric because he literally *cannot* grasp anybody else's point of view.

There have been many psychological investigations that confirm that children this age struggle to consider how other people think and feel. The typical toddler sees the world only from his point of view and he simply doesn't understand that other people may have a different perspective.

Try this

Sit your toddler in a chair at one end of a small table, then sit his favourite teddy in a chair at the opposite end – make sure that your toddler and the teddy are facing each other. Next, take a couple of small toys (for instance, a ball and a rubber duck) and put them side by side – exactly in the middle of the table – with the ball nearer to your toddler and the duck nearer to his teddy.

Then ask your child 'What toy does teddy see first, the ball or the duck?' He looks at the table, sees the ball before the duck, automatically thinks 'Teddy sees what I see', and tells you that his teddy also sees the ball first. This stage of egocentricity often lasts until around the age of three or four years.

You're like me

Your toddler's egocentricity affects him in other ways too. For instance, if he sees you upset, the chances are that he offers you his favourite cuddly toy in order to cheer you up. He does this because he thinks 'My teddy cheers me up when I am unhappy, so it will do the same for you.' He assumes that what works as a comfort for him will work for everyone.

Egocentricity is also responsible for 'animism', which is the phenomenon by which many young children think that everything in the world is alive, just like them. That's why your toddler tells you that 'the sun wakes up in the morning'. Likewise, he might cry genuine tears after dropping a cuddly toy on the floor because he really does think it feels pain, just as he does when he falls.

I'm furious

Tantrums are common in toddlers, largely because your two-year-old has not yet gained self-control. Due to her egocentricity, she sees the world only from her point of view and expects to be able to do whatever she wants.

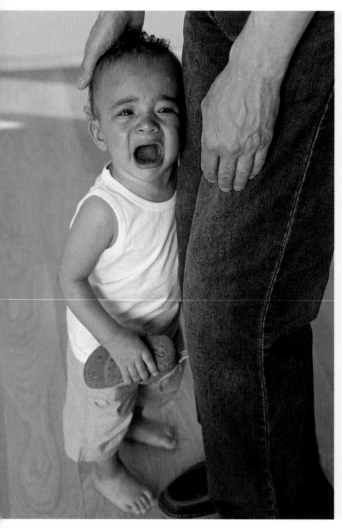

Facts about tantrums

■ The peak age for tantrums is between the ages of one and three years. Tantrums are equally common in boys and girls.

■ Toddlers raised by parents who let them do as they please are just as likely as any other toddler to have tantrums. They still have outbursts.

■ One study found that at least 48 per cent of toddlers hit out at others in temper or snatch things from them, while 64 per cent thump their sibling during a tantrum.

■ A toddler may have a breath-holding tantrum, in which she becomes so enraged that she involuntarily holds her breath until she faints.

■ During a temper tantrum a toddler is capable of hurting herself – in sheer frustration, she may throw herself on the floor or bang her head off a wall or table.

Get out of my way!

Your toddler is old enough to know that she has ideas of her own, but she's not yet mature enough to realize that other people have feelings too and that her wishes can't always come first in the queue. When she can't get her own way, she screams, shouts, rages (and maybe even kicks and hits). She thinks 'You're making me mad because you're standing in my way.' Her sense of self-importance is very strong, and she rages at anything which blocks her path.

I can get what I want

It's not just chance that your toddler has a furious outburst in a public place, such as the local supermarket or during a family gathering at your house. Tantrums occur more frequently at these times for two reasons.

First, your toddler is excited by the change in surroundings, and the more excited she is, the more volatile she becomes. Second, she has learned from experience that you are more likely to give in to her demands when there are others around: she recognizes that you find such moments embarrassing, that your will to resist her challenges is lower in public and that you want to appear competent in front of others. So, if you don't stand your ground, she soon thinks 'This is the best place to scream for a new toy', and you'll consequently find that her public tantrums increase dramatically.

I can't sit on this!

Don't be surprised when your toddler dashes off the potty the moment you sit him on it for the first time. He is so used to wearing nappies that sitting down without one covering his bottom makes him feel strange and perhaps even anxious.

I'm worried about this

You know that this is the normal position for toileting but he thinks 'This seems very strange to me.' He needs time to adjust to this new experience, because as far as he is concerned using a nappy is much more sensible than sitting on a seat!

Your toddler may also feel very vulnerable without his nappy on, as that usually only happens when he is getting washed or changed. Some toddlers even feel frightened when they first use the potty properly and then see what they have done in it.

DID YOU KNOW?

- You have the urge to use the toilet when your bladder is almost three-quarters full. Your toddler, however, automatically empties his bladder long before then.
- A toddler does not usually have sufficiently mature muscle and neurological systems to control his bowel and bladder until he is at least 15 months old.
- Boys are usually slower to acquire toilet control than girls, and this applies to both day and night. Scientists aren't sure why this gender difference exists.
- Almost 90 per cent of all children gain reliable control over their bowel and bladder during the day by the time they reach the age of three years.
- Your child gains bowel and bladder control during the day before he manages this at night. By three years, around 75 per cent of children have night-time control as well.

I'm ready

Your toddler will show signs that he is ready for potty training. If you start too early, battles may develop because you might become irritated with him, which in turn could make him feel bad for failing you.

The typical time for potty training to begin is around 20 months, give or take a couple of months either side. Your child's way of telling you 'I'm ready for potty training' is when:

- He lets you know that his nappy is wet or dirty (either by telling you or by pointing).
- He is aware that he is filling his nappy.
- You discover that his nappy is dry even though he has been wearing it for hours.

I like this

Your child participates enthusiastically in toilet training when:

- He is familiar with the potty and is used to sitting on it without wearing a nappy.
- He feels that you are happy with his achievements during toilet training.
- He thinks he has lots of time to use the potty, without feeling rushed.
- He doesn't feel rejected for any toileting 'accidents' that occur during training.
- He has fun while sitting on the potty, perhaps singing a song or listening to a story.
- He gets lots of praise from you every time he uses the potty properly.
- He sees that you are relaxed with him, not tense or frustrated by his slow progress.
- He is given plenty of time to develop his bowel and bladder control.
- He is allowed to wear trainer pants once he has had a few successes.

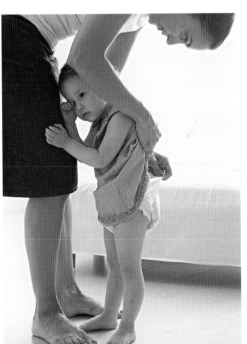

I'm not eating that!

The chances are that your infant or toddler will go through a phase of fussy eating, usually from the age of around 24 months (though it can start earlier). She thinks 'I've no intention of eating that' and either refuses to touch the food in front of her, or just sits picking at her plate with a terribly sad expression on her face.

You can't make me!

You cannot force your child to eat. If she misbehaves in other ways, you can do something immediate such as remove her toy or give her a reprimand. It's different with eating, however, because your toddler is totally in control of what she chews and swallows. No matter how much pressure you put on her, she has to make the choice to eat. And that's why methods of confrontation with your fussy eater don't work – co-operation is much more effective.

RESEARCH SHOWS

In one project, lasting several weeks and involving hundreds of children, the young eaters were allowed to eat whatever they wanted, whenever they wanted. Surprisingly, most children tried every food that was on offer and rarely did a child eat too much of anything. And there were no complaints of loss of appetite or sore tummies during this time. Qualified dieticians involved in the study agreed at the end that the food eaten by the children overall represented a balanced diet. It seems as though your toddler instinctively knows what to eat and what not to eat.

Choice – however minimal – is important to your toddler, though it's always best to make sure she picks from a range of healthy foods. She refuses to eat if she thinks 'She's forcing me.' Your toddler will eat happily when she thinks 'This is fun, relaxing and nobody is hassling me'.

I don't like that

- Many eating fads pass as quickly as they appear, although there are plenty of toddlers who consistently pick at their meals.
- Faddy eating habits are less common before the second year – less than one-tenth of parents are anxious about their one-year-olds' eating habits.
- Around one-fifth of parents are convinced that their toddlers aged two and three have poor appetites and that they are fussy eaters.
- This problem increases over the next year, so that by the age of four almost half of all parents express worry about their child's eating habits.
- Some eating habits have little to do with appetite – a toddler may refuse to eat her dinner and yet gulp down a chocolate bar immediately afterwards.

It doesn't look right

Look at the eating experience from your child's point of view:

- Is the cutlery the right size for her hands, and does her chair provide her with a comfortable seating position? She needs to feel at ease for eating.
- Is the portion size suitable? Putting too much on her plate may kill her appetite instantly.
- Is the food at the right temperature? If it is served too hot, she may be afraid of burning her mouth – and yet she may not have the patience to wait for it to cool.
- Does the food have the taste she likes? You might prefer foods with distinctive flavours, but children prefer much plainer fare.
- What is the texture of the food? Food that is too dry or too greasy can stick to her upper palate, making her sick.

I'm up for it

A confident toddler has a positive outlook on life. It's not that he's foolhardy or reckless, just that he believes in himself and his ability to do what is required in a variety of situations.

I've got attitude

If you have a child who is full of self-confidence, you'll find that he's relaxed and happy much of the time, rather than getting upset at life's little challenges – such as meeting new friends, tidying his room, learning new topics, or taking part in a new game in pre-school. He approaches these experiences optimistically, because he thinks 'No problem, this looks good fun.' And there is evidence from research that suggests young children with a confident attitude keep this outlook throughout childhood and into adulthood.

Encourage me

Your toddler takes a confident attitude when he:

Believes in himself. In other words, he believes in his abilities. New learning experiences don't worry him, because he thinks he has the necessary abilities to cope. This self-belief keeps his motivation strong, and each achievement boosts his confidence even higher.

Has high self-esteem. He values himself positively, which means that he thinks 'I believe I'm a good person.' It's not that he's big-headed: it's just that he likes himself and is proud of his attainments, whether socially, educationally or physically. He feels comfortable with who he is as an individual.

Has a good self-image. Your confident toddler is happy with himself because others react positively to him. Your approval when he completes a task or meets a challenge improves his self-image (the way he sees himself) because he feels you support and approve of him.

That's a help

Your toddler's positive outlook on himself is strengthened when he sees you taking an interest in everything he does, when you let him know how pleased you are with his progress and when you spend time with him whenever you can. He thrives on your praise, enthusiasm and encouragement. Another great boost to his positive attitude is success – the more often he achieves his target, the harder he tries to achieve at the next level. Success breeds success.

Sometimes a toddler has unrealistic expectations: his belief in himself outstrips his abilities, and his confidence comes crashing down when his fantasies meet reality. That's why, for instance, he gives up jigsaws entirely when he couldn't complete his older brother's 100-piece puzzle! He thrives best when his aims are at a realistic level.

When you say...

Your child's confidence is influenced strongly by language.

When you say...	He thinks...
'I think you are terrific.'	'That makes me feel good.'
'I'm going to tell grandma how you helped me.'	'I'm very proud.'
'I enjoy being with you.'	'I must be a nice child.'
'You are great at this.'	'I am quite clever.'
'You have so many friends.'	'Other children definitely like me.'
'Your brother is very proud of you.'	'I am so pleased.'
'You look very handsome today.'	'I am good-looking.'
'Let's put your painting here.'	'What I do is worthwhile.'

Chatterbox

That sounds interesting

You may wonder what your baby thinks when you speak to her. After all, she can't speak back to you and she certainly doesn't understand the meaning of the vast majority of words that you use. Yet the meaning is only one aspect of spoken language.

It's a social occasion

Your baby gets a lot more out of hearing you talk to her than that. First, there is the social dimension. Whenever you talk to your baby, you say something, look at her, pause, then say something else, as if taking part in a conversation where you are the only one who talks. As well as developing your baby's turn-taking skills (see pages 96–97), this also encourages her to think 'Talking is good fun' because she sees you smile and look at her while you speak. Second, your words carry a range of sounds, some of which she tries to make herself – she thinks 'I want to try to speak like you.' She is encouraged by you.

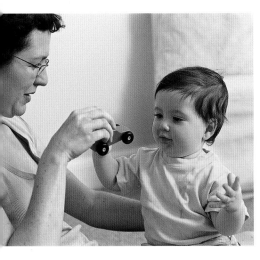

I like your tone

Adults often spontaneously change their tone and speech style when talking to a young baby: typically, they use a greater range of voice tones, shorter words and more animated facial expressions. Known as 'motherese' or 'parentese', this instinctive style of language is perfect for catching your baby's interest and attention.

She loves high tones and low tones in preference to monotones, she loves seeing very exaggerated facial expressions because they are easier for her to interpret, and she loves words that are short and easy to process. That's why she thinks 'This is great,' when you talk to her that way. Of course, you shouldn't do this all the time – make sure that you also talk to her in your normal voice, so she gradually tunes in to this too.

Read my face

Your baby communicates with you non-verbally, using body language. She tells you what she thinks and feels by changing the expression on her face, by using the limited range of sounds available to her (such as babbling, yelling, crying), and by moving her arms and legs (see pages 36–37).

You can help her develop this form of communication – which is a precursor to spoken language – by responding appropriately to her: for instance, soothing her when she cries, smiling back at her when she smiles at you, or waving you hands with excitement just as she does. When you are in tune with her body language, she thinks 'Yes, you understand me', and she feels secure and happy as a result.

DID YOU KNOW?

Psychologists use the term 'receptive language' to describe the speech and language a child understands, and the term 'expressive language' to describe the speech and language a child is able to produce herself. Both these aspects develop strongly during the first three years of life.

Right from birth, and continuing throughout childhood, receptive language exceeds expressive language. In other words, your young child always understands a lot more than she can say at any time. So when you talk to your baby using a range of common everyday words, she starts to learn their meaning by associating them with particular objects (for instance, you say 'teddy' when you hold up her teddy), even though she cannot actually utter the words herself.

My memories

Without memory, your child wouldn't learn language or indeed anything at all. For instance, watch your toddler search for his favourite cuddly toy – not only can he remember it from the last time, he can also remember where it might be. If he didn't have good recall, he wouldn't even look for the toy in the first place!

Is this useful?

Through memory, your infant gathers information, sorts it all out, decides what's worth keeping and what can be rejected, stores it, and then uses it whenever he wants. Your child's mind spontaneously decides what to remember and what to forget, then files the useful information in memory. When he wants to remember something, he is able to do so. Memory provides the building blocks on which his understanding and learning develop.

I remember

Within a few hours of birth, your baby reacts more strongly to sounds that he heard while in the womb than he does to new sounds (see pages 24–25). He thinks 'I've heard that before.' Just like you, your baby's memory is more effective with prompts. In one study, each three-month-old baby was taught to activate a mobile above his cot using his ankle. When shown the mobile two weeks later, the baby appeared to have forgotten how to make it move. But with a gentle prompt (the investigator moved the mobile), each baby thought 'Now I remember what to do' and began moving it himself.

How memory develops

From birth onwards, your growing infant has five different types of memory:

Visual He remembers sights (he recognizes your face, his favourite toy, his older sister, his bedroom wallpaper).

Auditory He remembers previously heard sounds (he chuckles when he hears you say his name gently, even if he can't see you at the time).

Olfactory This is a baby's memory for smells and tastes (he can differentiate the smell of his mother's milk from another mother's milk, see pages 26–27).

Kinesthetic Your baby is able to recall specific movements he has made (he soon learns that shaking the rattle causes it to make a noise).

Semantic Words and language play important parts in our lives, and semantic memory enables him to remember language and its meaning.

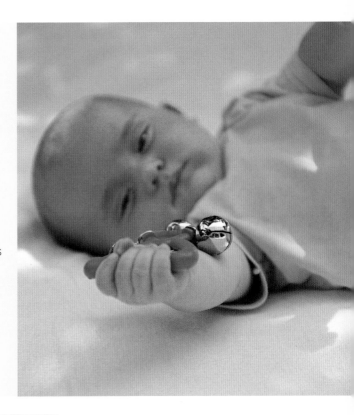

It's getting better

Your infant's memory improves steadily over the first two years, with your help. Hands-on involvement helps him to recall: for instance, he has a better chance of remembering a song or poem when he has been actively involved in saying it, instead of just listening to it. He thinks 'I remember this because I did it before.'

And he also remembers better when the memory has vivid associations. For instance, he finds it easier to remember a nursery rhyme if it is presented to him in a lively way – his interest helps his memory to be more efficient.

Practice is very important too. It's hard for your child to remember something he has done only once. Repetition and practice enable him to fix the experience more firmly in his mind.

Oo, Aa

By the age of two months, your baby begins to realize she can make more noises than simply screaming or crying. You'll notice that she makes these gurgling-type 'cooing' sounds (long vowels such as 'oo' and 'aa') when she is happy and playful. It's her way of telling you 'I feel good right now.'

I feel good

Compared to crying, cooing is more varied with a greater range of tones, enabling your baby to gradually extend her verbal abilities. Increased control over her vocal muscles also helps. Your baby coos at you because she feels comfortable and contented; she wants to let you know she is pleased. There is no other meaning behind these baby sounds. Although you might hear her make a cooing sound that remotely resembles a real word, that is only coincidence, so don't read too much into it.

Bibble, wibble, babble

It all starts to change at around six or seven months, when your infant moves from cooing to making babbling noises – distinctive sounds that are clear and are recognizable as individual syllables.

Most psychologists agree that a baby's first words – which don't appear until later – are based on these small units of babbled speech. Unlike cooing, babbling is purposeful and is your infant's way of practising her sounds in preparation for full speech later on. She first makes sounds using 'reduplicated babbling', in which she repeats the same consonant-vowel combination, such as 'lelelele', but by the age of 10 or 11 months this changes to 'variegated babbling', in which she puts together strings of different syllables, such as 'balukama'.

Babbling, though, is more for her benefit than yours: studies have found that a baby typically babbles more when she is alone than when an adult is with her.

I love this noise

Your baby also enjoys hearing the sounds of cooing and babbling, whether or not they have any meaning attached to them. She thinks 'These noises that I'm making are very interesting', and so she continues with them.

Evidence shows that even by the time she is only four months old, your baby can tell the difference between one babble syllable and another. For instance, one study of infants this age found that they became bored and disinterested (as assessed by their rate of sucking) when the same two consonant-vowel sounds were repeated, such as 'baa' and 'baa'. But when one aspect of these consonant-vowel units was subtly changed – for instance, to 'baa' and 'paa' – their rate of sucking noticeably increased. This proves that babies can clearly discriminate between these two sound combinations. Your baby likes these sounds so much that she often babbles herself to sleep or when she has just woken up in the morning.

RESEARCH SHOWS

Another advantage of babbling for your baby is that she can use it to draw you into basic conversation. Researchers found that babbling causes parents spontaneously to teach their infant conversational skills. What happens is that the baby's vocal responsiveness acts as positive feedback, which stimulates her parents' vocalizations. The parent assumes that the baby has genuine meaning underlying her language sounds (even though that might not be accurate), and so starts to talk to her using a more traditional style of conversation in which the baby babbles, the parent speaks, the baby then babbles again, each taking turns to contribute to this dialogue.

I'll show you what I mean

As your baby can't use spoken language to express himself at least until he says his first word (and he might not be able to voice his emotions until he is two or three years old), he uses non-verbal communication to convey his ideas and feelings to you.

Can you understand me?

Body language – the meaning your baby transmits to you through his body movements, such as gaze, facial expression, and touch – is an important channel of communication. Although the understanding of body language can be complex – estimates suggest there are more than one million different gestures and expressions that convey meaning – you will very quickly tune in to your infant's non-verbal communication (see also pages 36–37). When you accurately interpret his non-verbal messages and react appropriately to him, he thinks 'Great, now we are connecting with each other', and is delighted.

How body language develops

At the toddler stage, your child starts to combine non-verbal gestures, allowing a more sophisticated use of body language. Here are some of the typical thoughts and feelings he conveys using these 'clusters':

'I can do it myself.' When he moves away from you and moans while attempting a difficult challenge, he is insisting that he is independent.

'I'm feeling frustrated.' It is frustration that causes him to cry and then throw his toy against the floor. He releases tension through arm, leg and hand gestures.

'I want you to be my friend.' When your toddler wants to be friends with another child, he moves over beside them and stares happily into their face.

Look at my face

Your baby expresses seven basic emotions through his facial expression:

'I'm unhappy.' His lower lip pouts, his eyes wrinkle up, his chin quivers – he's thoroughly miserable.

'I'm happy.' With eyes wide open and sparkling, coupled with gurgling noises and a big smile – he's very happy.

'I'm surprised.' When experiencing this emotion, your baby's eyes and mouth are wide open, and his brow has deep furrows.

'I'm fascinated.' If interested, his eyes narrow, he tries to lean forward, and his gaze is unflinching.

'I'm disgusted.' He expresses this feeling by stretching his mouth open lengthwise and wrinkling his eyes.

'I'm afraid.' Fear is expressed facially through a half-opened mouth, arms held tight to his body, and his eyes partly closed.

'I'm angry.' The sight of his red face, lined brow and rapid breathing informs you immediately that he's furious.

I like cuddles

Gentle touch between you and your baby is frequent in the early months of life, but tails off towards the end of the second year. There are developmental reasons for this. First, your toddler's independence means that you don't have to hold him when feeding, and you don't have to carry him everywhere. Second, he now exercises choice about cuddling – he moves away from you if he doesn't want a hug.

But this reduction of touch as a spontaneous form of non-verbal communication actually increases its emotional significance for your toddler. Since cuddles, hugs and other loving gestures are no longer an essential part of his life, they are even more special now when they do occur. For instance, stroking his face gently when he plays peacefully with his toys for a while makes him beam with delight.

I'm learning to talk

Your baby's babbling eventually progresses towards her first word. Babbling is part of the preparation – you may notice that around the age of nine or ten months, her babbling takes on an intonation that resembles the tone and style of the language she hears from you. It's almost as if she is learning the tune before she learns the words themselves.

It's all in the tone

Babies usually have two babbling 'tunes', one that goes up at the end (which suggests she is thinking 'Now it's your turn') and one that goes down at the end (which suggests she is thinking 'That's all I've got to say on the matter'). Also at this stage in her development, your infant's babbling becomes much closer to the range of sounds that you use. It is almost as if she is preparing specifically to say her first word to you.

Mama! Dada!

Her first word – usually uttered around 12 months – need not conform exactly to a word that you use. Bear in mind that your infant's first word is any sound (or combination of sounds) that she uses consistently to refer to the same object. So if she says 'lapa' every time you appear, the chances are she thinks 'That's my mother.' The most common first words are 'mama' and 'dada', although not always. These tend to be recognized as an infant's first word because you listen out for them, because each of these words is easy for her to say, and because you probably say these words to her regularly in the hope that she will repeat them. The transition from babbling to speaking is a gradual process that spans a period of months rather than weeks.

Look who's talking!

After the excitement generated by your toddler's first word dies down, you may be disappointed that the growth in her vocabulary is surprisingly slow during subsequent months. This is normal. A toddler who says her first word at one year typically only uses between 30 and 50 words six months later. Psychologists assume this occurs because your toddler thinks the word applies only to a specific object ('doggie' for the family dog), not realizing that the word symbolizes a range of objects ('doggie' for every dog in the world). At 18 months, however, there is a 'naming explosion', in which there is a huge surge in the rate at which she acquires new words. Estimates suggest that her vocabulary now increases at an average rate of six words a day.

What *exactly* is that?

The way toddlers extend their single-words vocabulary reveals a great deal about their thinking skills. For instance, in the early stages of speaking your child may use the word 'tat' to indicate your family cat and also whenever he sees any animal that walks on four legs, such as a dog, horse or cow. The moment this over-extension stops and she confines her use of 'tat' to cats, you know that she now understands the conceptual category of 'cats'. That's a big step forward in her thought processes.

Sometimes your toddler creates new words of her own that she has never heard used before (such as 'gonded' to indicate that someone has left the room) – this is a very positive sign which confirms she is beginning to use language creatively and purposefully.

My own words

From the age of 12–18 months, your toddler at times uses one word as if it is an entire sentence. For instance, when he points to a cup of juice that has spilled on the floor and says 'Juice', what he really means is 'My juice has spilled on the floor.'

One word will do

You might not always understand the full intention of these single-word utterances and this can frustrate your toddler, but do what you can to interpret them accurately. Between 18 and 24 months, he moves on to using two-word sentences. Research suggests that he doesn't start talking in phrases and sentences until his vocabulary contains at least 100 words.

I can speak properly

Your toddler has a vocabulary explosion at 18 months – and a grammar explosion around 12 months later. His language skills improve rapidly now. What he says is much closer to what he thinks. The telegraphic nature of his speech disappears as he includes lots of smaller words such as 'and', 'but', 'my' and 'am'. Very quickly he starts to use plurals, past tenses, prepositions and other minor grammatical structures. Instead of just nouns and verbs, your toddler speaks using a broad range of constructions, making his speech more closely resemble yours. He also starts to use inflections (that is, he raises his voice at the end of a phrase to indicate it is an enquiry) – for instance, 'Where teddy?'

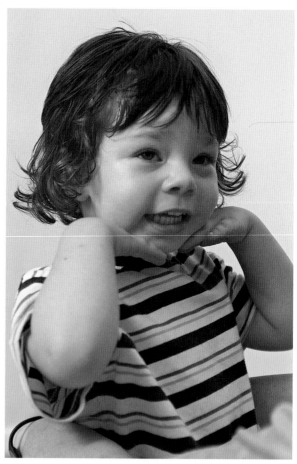

First sentences

Your toddler's first sentences have a number of distinct features:

They are short. He moves from single words to phrases that are two or three words long. However, by the age of two years he is using sentences with up to four or five words, and when he is 30 months his sentences contain up to ten words.

They are telegraphic. Just as the telegrams of the past used only essential words and missed out smaller words, your toddler talks in the same way. He says 'Me want ball' instead of 'I want the ball.'

They follow rules. For instance, you can predict he'll say 'Daddy chair' when he means to say 'That's daddy's chair'. He uses the same rules for speaking each time.

That's what I'm saying

There are so many changes in your child's speech by the time he reaches his third birthday that they are too extensive to list. Many of them are to do with the way he uses tone, emphasis and intonation in order to change subtly the meaning of the words. When, for instance, he sees that his teddy is broken he thinks 'My teddy is broken, not my chair or my bed, but my teddy.' He knows that stressing one word in a sentence is an effective way of drawing attention to this, so he is able to convey the very specific meaning using fewer words combined with emphasis. By saying 'My teddy is broken', he tells you exactly what he means.

Once your child starts to talk in sentences, you might notice him having a conversation with someone who isn't there – maybe even offering them his toys to play with or a drink from his beaker. That's his imaginary friend, a phenomenon that's so common during the pre-school years that psychologists consider it a normal part of child development. Don't worry – he knows his imaginary friend doesn't exist. The presence of his 'friend' is not a sign of loneliness or sadness: it is simply a way of making his day more interesting through the use of his imagination.

Let's sing!

Songs and music play an important part in your child's life, serving a number of different purposes. As a baby, her relationship with singing is passive – she likes to listen because she can't sing along. Since you tend to sing to her when you want to soothe or calm her, while holding her close to your body, songs gradually become associated in her mind with pleasant feelings, relaxation and warmth.

Sing me to sleep

Your child hears you sing and thinks 'You're here and that makes me feel safe and secure.' That's why lullabies are so effective. As far as you are concerned, you might think you have a dreadful singing voice, yet your baby totally disagrees – to her ears, the sound of your singing is the most wonderful music in the world, and she very quickly falls asleep in the process.

I'll sing too

From the age of 12 months or so, your infant tries to join in with your singing. She makes an attempt to mimic the tune, even though her sounds don't match the words. She wants to do what you do; her face lights up when she hears you sing a familiar song.

By the end of her second year, she likes you to sing the line of a song but miss out the last word, giving her the opportunity to fill in the empty space – her vocabulary skills and memory are strong enough for her to manage this. And soon after that she makes a reasonable attempt to sing the actual words herself. It's not until the age of two or three years that you can clearly recognize the songs she sings. Your toddler especially loves songs that involve actions as well as words.

Let's move!

Familiar nursery rhymes tend to be very popular with young children, probably because they have lots of repetition and lots of interaction. For instance, 'This little piggy' uses the same words over and over, while finishing with you tickling her along her body and up her arms. Once she is familiar with this rhyme, she starts to giggle as soon you as you say the first line because she thinks 'I know she's going to tickle me in a minute.'

Other nursery rhymes and songs require full body movements, such as 'Incy wincy spider' or 'Ring-a-ring-o'-roses'. The more actions and words involved the better. You may find that she wants you to repeat the same rhyme over and over until she can manage to say the words by herself.

How reading skills help

Knowledge of nursery rhymes and the ability to recite them may be linked to the acquisition of reading skills. A study looked at a large number of children at three years old and assessed the number of nursery rhymes they knew. A few years later, the investigators looked at the same children's reading skills and the ease with which they had learned to read. The results showed that children who had known more nursery rhymes when they were three years old had greater awareness of sounds and learned to read more easily, compared to those who had known fewer rhymes at that age. It looks as though experience of nursery rhymes during the toddler years boosts your child's thinking skills in a way that enhances her ability to learn to read.

Chat, chat, chat

Your toddler learns anything (including language) more easily when he is relaxed and having fun, so make a point of chatting to him during routine daily activities. He models his own speech to a large extent on yours and thinks 'I'm going to learn to speak like you.' So chat freely while you play with him, change him, and take him on outings with you.

Are you listening to me?

Although the meaning of your child's vocalizations is not entirely clear in the first couple of years, make a show of listening anyway. Do your best to look at him when he talks to you, and try to make an appropriate response. He thrives on your attention.

That makes a change

For your toddler, variety can be the spice of life. True, he likes familiar routines (see pages 40–41), but he also likes to experience new activities.

Try to develop a range of language stimulation exercises. For instance, in addition to songs and rhymes you can also read stories to him – he just adores staring at story books while you read. Let him snuggle close, suggest that he points to the pictures as they are mentioned in the story, and vary your voice tone to match the content and theme of the story.

And give him a toy telephone. Your two-year-old enjoys having an imaginary conversation, perhaps 'phoning' his grandmother or his best friend. Once he gets started, you'll have a hard time getting him to stop!

How speech develops

A young child tends to use one of two styles of speech. He may use words in an expressive style, in order to describe or enhance social relationships (such as 'please', 'thank you' and 'yes'), or in a referential style, in order to name specific objects (such as 'grandma', 'dog' and 'cup'). Researchers have found that toddlers who predominantly use an expressive style are more interested in people and social interactions; they typically use longer strings of words and their language often appears quite advanced. However, they tend to have smaller vocabularies. In contrast, toddlers with a referential style tend to be more solitary and more interested in objects than in people; they usually have a much greater range of words and are more able to understand adult language.

From the age of around two years onwards, your child starts to ask you lots of questions. He realizes this is a great way to acquire new information – and also to grab your attention, so don't be surprised with his endless list of enquiries. Treat them seriously and answer as best you can. Through your positive responses, your toddler thinks 'This is a great way for me to learn more', and it encourages his enquiring mind.

I'll try that again

Expect your toddler to make plenty of mistakes while he improves his speech and language. He mixes up words sometimes, mispronounces initial letter sounds from time to time, and even makes up words that he's never heard you use before. Don't correct him when he makes these sorts of mistakes, or he may think 'I'll just keep quiet rather than be told off again.' Instead, say the correct words and phrases yourself, as if you are agreeing with him rather than pointing out his mistake. For instance, if he watches a bird fly away and says 'Birdie gonded' you could say 'Yes, that's right. The bird has flown away.'

Index

Acknowledgements

Thank you to all the parents and children who attended the photo shoots for this book: Megan Bradley; Alexa and Sacha Congreave; Mary and Emma Craig; Michelle Hale and Chloe Fackerell; Chie and Shelly Gordon; Julie and Adam Grimes; Paul, Penny, Louis and Freddie Hannam; Katie and Willoughby Hardwicke; Nicola Hendey; Christine Henry; Rachel Green and Philip Jones; Annabel, Amber and Mathilde King; Katie and Danny Knowles; Sofia May Leeson; Shaun and Freddie McGrath; Shirley McIntosh; Julia and Oscar McKay; Mirka Miturova; Jemma Jessup and Jaya Morrison; Tess Partington; Katy Linfield and Billie Powell; Caroline Pole and Harry Randall; Nikki, Bea and Mabel Simms; Sian Dodds and Lauren Strand; Rhonda and Adam Summersbell; Brett and Ellie Thorburn; Claire Wedderburn-Maxwell and Amelia Thorpe; Julia and Millie Twelftree; Anja and Isabella Valentic; Kate and Evie-May Walsh; Claire and Asha White; and Chris, Elizabeth and Alice Wilson.

Picture acknowledgements

Special Photography: © Octopus Publishing Group Limited/Russell Sadur.

Other Photography: BananaStock 13 bottom, 36 centre right, 41 top left, 43 bottom right, 85 top left. **Corbis UK Ltd**/Lester Lefkowitz 18 centre right. **Octopus Publishing Group Limited**/Adrian Pope 31 bottom, 40 bottom right, 41 bottom right, 56 bottom left, 70 bottom right, 76, 114, 129; /Peter Pugh-Cook 46, 48. **Photodisc** 8, 27 bottom, 103 bottom left.

Executive Editor Jane McIntosh
Managing Editor Clare Churly
Design Manager Tokiko Morishima
Picture Library Manager Jennifer Veall
Picture Librarian Sophie Delpech
Designer Maggie Town, one2six creative
Photographer Russel Sadur
Production Assistant Nosheen Shan